Valerie Sims

Vintage
Norman Island

True Treasure Tales

Discover Norman Island's History!

*True Tales About a Real Treasure Island
with Pirates and Buried Treasure in the
British Virgin Islands*

+150 Rare Photographs

Valerie Sims

A Creque Family Memoir

Vintage Norman Island

First Edition
ISBN: 978-1-7343863-1-8

Printed in the United States of America

Published by:
Vintage World Media SEZC,
P.O. Box 550, Cruz Bay, St. John
US Virgin Islands, 00831

Copyright Information

No part of this manuscript may be reproduced, stored in a retrieval system, or transmitted in any form or by any means, electronic, mechanical, photocopying, recording, or otherwise, without the written permission from the copyright holder set out within.

To do so is an infringement of copyright law.

For Book Purchases

For more information or to purchase, please visit NormanIslandbook.com. Quantity books are available for educational use or as corporate gifts.

Author's Note

This book is a work of nonfiction. It is based on many interviews with the people who experienced the events told within, as well as research in various archives, including out-of-print newspapers, personal diaries, and letters.

Memory and history are subjective, and any work of literary nonfiction has an element of subjectivity as well. I have done my best to adhere to the truth as my sources believe it to be throughout this book.

The ideas and perspectives expressed within do not necessarily reflect the author's opinion.

Disclaimer: Neither the publisher nor the author shall be held liable or responsible for any loss or damage allegedly arising from any suggestion or information contained in this book.

Please note that Norman Island is a private island.

Cover Photograph

The necklace on the cover was assembled with nine Spanish dollars reportedly found in a cave at Norman Island. Henry O. Creque gave them to his wife, Margaret 'Peggy' Creque during the mid-1950s. The necklace remains in the family to this day. The image on the back cover of Long John Silver is licensed from Alamy.com.

A Gift to You

FREE bonus material is available for you as a gift to thank you for your purchase. Visit: valeriesims.info/bonus

Dedications

To my mother: You are my biggest fan and fun companion on all my treasure hunting adventures! As you know, Mom, writing this book was a labor of love. Thank you for all your help and inspiration along the way. I couldn't have done it without you!

To the descendants of Henry and Maria Creque: Your ancestors loved their lands so much that they recorded the island's history for you through the photographs they took, the documents and letters they saved, and the entries they submitted to the local newspapers.

They left a wonderful legacy to treasure! Without their collections, this manuscript could never have been written.

This Book is for You Too...

Belongers • British Virgin Islanders • Residents • Charter yacht and Hotel Guests • Researchers • Educators • Tour guides • Sailors Pirate Enthusiasts • Historians • US Virgin Islanders • Day Visitors Captains • History Buffs … and all those who contribute towards making the British Virgin Islands the special place it is today.

Additional Books by the Author and her Family

Vintage St. John: Discover St. John's History Through Seven Generations of Heartfelt Stories, Valerie Sims

Poems from a Small Island, Valerie Creque-Mawson

Persecuted and Prosecuted, Leon A. Mawson

Childhood Memories of Main Street, Marlene M. Mawson

STIGMA: Start to Imagine Giving More Acceptance, Leslie Carney

Island Boy Books, Arnold van Beverhoudt

Table of Contents

Henry Osmond Creque
Purchased Norman Island in 1896

*When asked about buried treasure,
Henry O. Creque, who reportedly found his wealth
in one of the caves, once remarked*
...

"You could be standing on it and never know it."

An Introduction

Vintage Norman Island is a collection of fascinating stories about the history of Norman Island and the hunt for hidden treasures.

Romantic tales of buried treasure and pirate lore have been associated with Norman Island since the beginning of recorded history.

In fact, the first documented discovery of buried treasure on the island took place in the year 1750, when the neighboring people of Tortola found it, and *'made a fine harvest of it.'*

Another significant discovery was made during the late nineteenth century, this one in the ceiling of the southern-most cave. A chiseled-out cavity 30-feet above sea level was the only evidence that pirates once hid something of value there.

When a merchant of St. Thomas appeared to become rich overnight, rumours spread that he discovered his wealth in this cave, but it's been a long-held family secret.

What Henry Osmond Creque found was never publicly revealed, fueling a century of speculation. H.O. Creque is the author's maternal great-great-grandfather.

Attempting to document exactly what he might have uncovered and when has been difficult with the passing of time, but interesting new clues have recently surfaced that may authenticate the rumours.

At fourteen years of age, when most boys were happy to spend time with their friends, Henry had other interests. He loved the excitement at live auctions and became one of its youngest bidders. One day, when the auctioneer's gavel struck, Henry became the owner of thirty acres of *Carrot Bay Estate* on the island of Tortola.

At fifteen, Henry was again the highest bidder for a lush estate with over two hundred and forty acres. This property included the beautiful beach known as *Cane Garden Bay*.

It's one of the most popular north shore beaches, nestled in a horseshoe-shaped harbour.

These two land transactions raise questions about how an ambitious teenager could afford to make such a purchase, but Henry's desire for acreage only grew.

He became enamored with Norman Island, Pelican Island, Flanagan Island, and the Peter Island Bight. He believed that Norman Island and Peter Island were perfect for both the establishment of coaling stations and the cultivation of cotton.

At the turn of the century, the use of coal as a fuel source provided a cheap and efficient source of power for transatlantic steamships. Henry felt that the islands' locations made them more advantageous for these services than neighboring islands in the Caribbean.

Now, six generations later, with access to private family files, extensive research, and copies of century-old manuscripts, a vivid picture of the history of Norman Island has emerged like never before.

Interwoven throughout these stories, you'll find a few surprising gems. Get ready to be transported back to a nostalgic time when provisioning passing ships was a viable business, and the hope of finding hidden treasure, a likely reality.

Thank you for your interest in Norman Island's past!

I hope you have a new reverence and appreciation for the history, splendor, and magnetism of this little remarkable island plagued by piracy.

Norman Island

A map of Norman Island in the British Virgin Islands

The British Virgin Islands

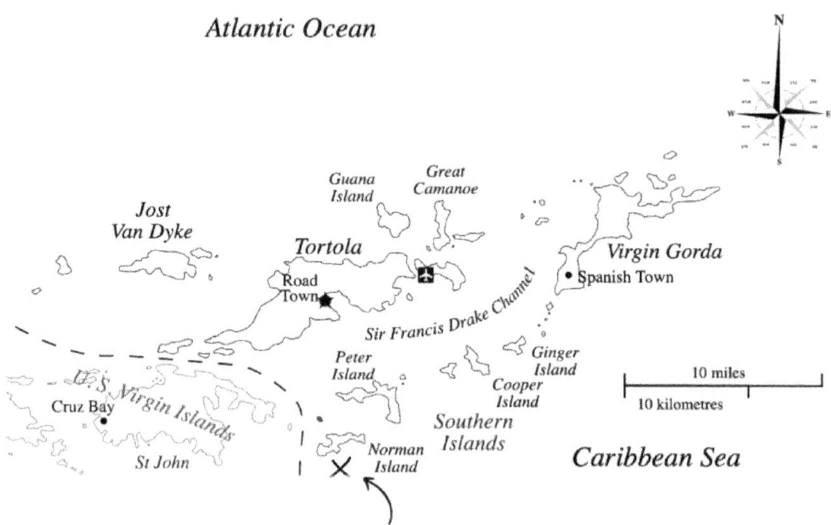

A Description of the Island

Norman Island is believed to be the ninth largest island in the British Virgin Islands, nestled in the vibrant blue waters of the West Indies. Its circumference is about 3 miles, containing over 620 acres, and lies fifteen miles due east of St. Thomas. The isle is reputed to be the inspiration behind Robert Louis Stevenson's *Treasure Island.*

Located astride the Sir Francis Drake Channel, one of the finest sailing grounds in the world, Norman Island is also one of the most popular yachting destinations in the Caribbean.

The Sir Francis Drake Channel was once known as the *Virgin's Gangway* or *Freebooters' Gangway* until it was renamed in honor of Drake, the most renowned privateer of the Elizabethan Age.

Sir Francis Drake

In 1585, Sir Francis Drake, along with 1,800 men, were rumoured to have anchored in the Bight before they sailed on to capture the city of Santo Domingo.

Their visit may have been the reason Soldier's Bay and Privateer's Bay were aptly named.

Sir Francis Drake

Infamous captains like William Kidd, "Black Sam" Bellamy, and Blackbeard also frequented these waters, dashing into secret coves and inlets to hide their nefarious activities. The rocky bluffs that abound were the perfect hideaway for them.

At the northwestern end of the island, there's a promontory called Treasure Point, where three musty caves open to the sea.

The largest cave extends about seventy feet into the mountainside, allowing snorkelers and small dinghies inside to explore. It twists around into a narrow chamber where a copper chest with over 200 coins was found in 1965.

Nearby, at Privateer's Bay, the land rises steeply to 440-feet at the highest summit on the island. At its peak, a breathtakingly beautiful view awaits the adventurous explorer.

Along these slopes, huge turpentine trees with red columns grow in profusion. Their paper-thin bark peels away in the scorching sun like a painful sunburn.

Did you know that a red-columned tree was the principal marker to the location where £700,000 in gold lay buried in *Treasure Island?*

Perhaps a legendary treasure still awaits discovery under one of their spreading shadows.

For Whom was Norman Island Named?

There are countless stories about how and for whom Norman Island was named, making it difficult to know with certainty.

- In 1997, Arnold R. Highfield, a local historian and author, translated J.L. Carstens', *St. Thomas in Early Danish Times*. Carstens' 1740 manuscript provided the earliest written perspective.

  Carstens research led him to believe that "Norman Island was named for a Danish man who was called, 'Nord Mand'. He was an inhabitant and planter on the nearby island of St. Thomas.

  'Nord Mand' reportedly moved to Norman Island with his enslaved workers and his furnishings to cultivate the island."

  If this supposition was true, 'Nord Mand' would have to have lived on the island many years prior to 1737. That's when Governor John Hart granted the entire island to its first recorded owner, Colonel Francis Phipps.

- Hamilton Cochran, the author of *These are the Virgin Islands*, (1937) published an interesting letter written from a gentleman planter of Tortola in 1760 to his brother in Britain.

  This letter described the buccaneers who freely used the Sir Francis Drake Channel. The tale he shared was very similar to that of the money diggers. It read:

  "Norman, a buccaneer, for whom the island may be named, separated himself from his associates, then in force on the island of Anegada, and settled with his portion of the general booty on this Cay."

"When the news reached Puerto Rico, Spanish Guarda Costas were ordered up the channel to sink, burn, and destroy all the freebooters they encountered.

In a conflict of this nature, Norman and his followers allegedly perished, not however, until they had deposited their hoard in that secret strong box, *the earth.*"

- There was a similar interpretation found in *Letters from the Virgin Islands,* which was published by an unknown author. (1843)

- George T. Eggleston, author of *Virgin Islands*, (1959) concurred that, "Norman Island was named for a pirate skipper who had a one-man kingdom on the island, hence the name Norman's Retreat. For many years, he preyed upon the shipping that passed through the Sir Francis Drake Channel."

There's no doubt that Norman Island's past is steeped in mystery and pirate legends.

Perhaps the origin of its name is not as important as its contribution to the history and beauty of the British Virgin Islands.

A cut ¼ dollar of a Piece-of-Eight

Chapter 1

The Legend of Norman Island

Margaret 'Peggy' Creque, wearing a treasured necklace, aged 23 in 1955. © Bill Creque

A Quest to Find the Truth

Have you ever been told a family secret that you thought was too far-fetched to be true? Did you try to research it further?

Ever since I was a young girl, I've been capturing the most incredible stories told to me by my grandmother and close relatives.

On a quest to find the truth about the treasures found on Norman Island, I implored a family member to help me find out fact from fiction. Little did I know, it would be the beginning of a fascinating journey through six generations of Norman Island's history!

Margaret 'Peggy' Creque

Margaret 'Peggy' Creque (1932-2017) was the third wife of Henry Ogilvie Creque, (1912-1957) my great-uncle. Peggy was an attractive, soft-spoken woman with a keen eye for business.

By the summer of 1957, tragic events turned her world upside-down when she became a widow at twenty-five. She suddenly had three small children to raise, as well as five of her late husband's offspring from his first marriage.

Those early years of widowhood were challenging and may have contributed to her strength of character and her no-nonsense approach to business.

After her husband's death, she managed the day-to-day operations of his business, a Chevrolet automobile dealership in the heart of St. Thomas. In the 1960s, women were expected to stay at home, but Peggy was determined to carry on, if not for herself, then for her children.

When I first became interested in genealogy, I appealed to Aunt Peggy to share her knowledge about our family's history with me.

Peggy's grandfather-in-law purchased Norman Island in 1896.

Ever since, whispers of a secret treasure Henry Osmond Creque found in one of the caves have been passed from ear to ear. Yet, to date, no one in the family had confirmed or documented the details surrounding this mystery.

Peggy was the last survivor of my grandmother's generation and the only relative alive who would know the true story behind the family rumours that have persisted for generations.

Henry Osmond Creque
(1858-1915)

Henry O. Creque was also my maternal great-great-grandfather, a fascinating man, whose life I've been researching for many years.

He was a British subject, born in 1858 in the Settlement, a tiny village-like town on the remote island of Anegada.

As the fifth child of seven, he was self-disciplined and industrious from a very early age.

Peggy's late husband was named after his Anegadian grandfather, who died in 1915. Henry was three years old and obviously had no memory of his grandfather, but he shared a very close relationship with his dad, Herman O. Creque.

Herman, being the only child of his father's marriage, had first-hand knowledge of what his father allegedly discovered. He likely told that tale to his five children.

My grandmother knew something of his find and shared a few tantalizing tidbits with me during an overnight visit to her house in the 1970s. But I wanted to know what Aunt Peggy knew of this mystery, since she was married to my grandmother's brother.

Henry O. Creque (1912–1957) Peggy Creque's husband, St. Thomas, US Virgin Islands

Talk of Hidden Treasure was Hush-Hush

I never met Uncle Henry because he passed away before I was born, so I spoke to Aunt Peggy when I could. However, she was always very allusive, prompting me to believe she knew more than she was willing to share. The funny thing about finding hidden treasure was, ... *Everyone in the family was always so hush-hush about it!*

I couldn't understand why, when local writers and visiting authors to the Virgin Islands had no hesitation in publishing stories about our family for decades.

In 1937, Hamilton Cochran, the author of *These are the Virgin Islands,* for instance, wrote that "a merchant of St. Thomas, who bought the island years ago for a cattle estate, found the treasure by accident after a heavy rain had exposed the cache."

In 1959, George T. Eggleston, the author of *Virgin Islands*, shared, "just after the turn of the last century, an impoverished Virgin Islander named Creque made a systematic search of the caves and found a treasure chest. The well-heeled Creque family are prominent merchants in St. Thomas to this day." Others have perpetuated the rumour that when descendants of Mr. Creque are betrothed, a necklace of Spanish doubloons is presented to the lucky bride.

Norman Island's Hidden Treasures

Below are the earliest published accounts of hidden treasure found on Norman Island.

- First, in November 1750, fifty chests of silver were brought to a secret bay and divided up among the crew before most of the individual shares were buried.

- Then, in 1880, a rumour surfaced in the local newspaper that treasure was found on the island.

- In 1889, a detailed article in a U.S. newspaper spoke convincingly of an earlier discovery around 1859.

- In 1905, Henry O. Creque was said to have found his wealth in one of the caves.

- More recently, in 1965, four visitors on a chartered yacht also made a surprise discovery in one of the caves. They retrieved a small copper chest with ancient coins, gemstones, and a crucifix.

Rarely can an island boast of having at least four hidden treasures, possibly more!

Some of these incredible stories have also been reprinted in various books and magazines throughout the years.

Following is another tantalizing example written by the author, Jill Tattersall of Tortola.

Her story was published in a 1989 Mapes Monde reprint of Robert Louis Stevenson's, *Treasure Island*.

The Legend of Norman Island

"Until early in this century, she wrote, a persistent rumour began to spread that an Anegada fisherman had been sheltering from heavy rain in a cave on Norman Island.

"When lighting a torch to keep off the fish-eating bats, he noticed a ledge on which a heap of rocks had collapsed, as if an earth tremor had dislodged them. Among the rocks, he saw an iron chest and several rotting leather bags.

"The fisherman did not go home to Anegada but sailed straight down to St. Thomas where he bought a large warehouse and prospered — as do his descendants to this day.

"A long time afterwards, a lady who had married into the family was asked if there was any truth to the legend of the treasure cave.

"She gave a Mona Lisa smile and said: *'We don't talk about it in the family, but I will tell you that on my wedding day, my father-in-law gave me a necklace of Spanish gold doubloons that hung down to my knees!'"*

When I read Jill Tattersall's account, I knew she was referring to Aunt Peggy, but there was just one problem. Peggy never met her father-in-law.

Herman O. Creque died in January 1949, three years before Peggy first visited the Virgin Islands. Despite this oversight, I believed there was some truth interwoven into her story, because I was told a similar tale as a youngster.

The question was... *How much truth was there?* Curious, I then began a lifelong quest to find the answer. Did Henry Osmond Creque discover a secret treasure in one of the caves? You're about to find out!

The Pieces-of-Eight Necklace

The necklace Jill referred to was likely the one pictured on the book's cover. Although it didn't extend to Peggy's knees as reported, it was remarkable, nonetheless.

Sally, Henry's youngest daughter with his first wife, shared her memories of seeing the necklace for the first time in the 1950s. After dinner one evening, as the family lingered around the table, her father presented the necklace to Peggy as a gift. When he clasped it around her delicate neck, everyone watched in awe as her upper body buckled under its weight, unexpectedly plunging her forward towards the table.

No one expected the necklace to be so heavy, not even Peggy! The nine Pillar dollars used in its design originated from Mexico City and were about 1.5 inches in diameter.

- Three of the silver coins were in the image of King Charles IV, and the remaining six were in the image of his son, Ferdinand VII.

- On the reverse was an engraving of Spain's royal coat of arms, the *Pillars of Hercules.*

- The dates ranged from 1803 to 1819.

These coins were some of the last currencies produced before the onset of the *Mexican War of Independence* and the closing of the mines.

Interestingly, there were four different assayer marks found on the collection: I.I., T.H., H.I., and F.T. The latter, 'F.T.,' represented Antonio Forcada y la Plaza. Silver platters, candlesticks, and beautiful chalices attributed to him can still be found today, two hundred years later, commanding a high price in the marketplace.

Peggy Creque's Necklace

A Brief History of the Pillar Dollar

The Pillar Dollar used in the necklace's design was America's first Silver Dollar.

It was the coin upon which the original United States dollar was based in the early nineteenth century and was officially recognized as legal tender.

Spanish dollars were widely circulated throughout the Caribbean, and some countries counter-marked them and used them as their local currency.

In Tortola and other places, they were cut into eight pieces to make small change, which was sorely needed.

A cut ¼ dollar of a Piece-of-Eight

According to Giorgio Migliavacca's article, *The Beautiful and Mysterious Coins of the British Virgin Islands*, after 1805, private entrepreneurs reproduced the very popular Tortola coins by counter-marking them, deliberately misspelling the word, Tortola to *Tirtila*.

This was done to avoid copyright infringement of the official coins. The strategy worked. The Treasury ultimately accepted these counter-stamped coins, which continued to be in circulation throughout the Virgin Islands and beyond.

Caribbean Pirates Active in the Early 1800s

If the Spanish dollars from Peggy's necklace were found in one of the caves and were part of a larger cache, then there were at least two Caribbean pirates who could have been responsible for their secretion; Roberto Cofresi, and Charles Gibbs.

1. Roberto Cofresi was considered the dominant Caribbean pirate of the era. He was born on the island of Puerto Rico and was active from 1818 to 1825, operating around St. Thomas and the neighboring islands.

    Considered the last of the successful West India pirates, he avoided capture by the navies of six nations for years, before becoming the ultimate target of an anti-piracy operation.

    After being captured by the Puerto Rican militia, he claimed to have a hidden stash of 4,000 pieces-of-eight, which he tried to use as a bribe.

    In 1825, the firing squad executed Cofresí and most of his crew. However, four *'evil-minded'* members of his gang were found hiding in St. Thomas the following year. They were swiftly captured and transported back to Puerto Rico.

"No pirates can have the least hope of avoiding the consequences of their misdeeds by shifting their residence from one colony to another," the newspapers reported.

Interestingly, the memory of *El Pirata Cofresí*, as he is known today, is romanticized on his native island.

Cofresi is considered a national hero, a Robin Hood figure who robbed from the rich and gave to the poor.

2. Charles Gibbs, on the other hand, was an American pirate born under the name of James D. Jeffers. He was cruel, more so than any other pirate of his day. Gibbs was a native of Rhode Island and was active in the Caribbean during the years 1816 to 1831, when the coins in Peggy's necklace may have been hidden.

"At about 15 years of age, Gibbs felt an inclination to roam. Like too many unreflecting youths of that age, he had a great fondness for the sea. In opposition to the friendly counsel of his parents, he secretly left and joined a sloop-of-war.

Gibbs admitted to privateering around 1816, and took part in a mutiny, after which, he turned to piracy full-time. "

"He possessed not the tender feelings to be operated upon by the shrieks and expiring groans of his devoted victims whom he casually threw overboard, whether they were dead or alive." His motto was, *"Dead men can tell no tales!"*

Overall, his confessions involved him in the robbery of over forty vessels and he participated in the murder of nearly 400 human beings!

When under the gallows, he confessed to being guilty of shedding the blood of many of his fellow men, but despite this revelation, he openly prayed for his own forgiveness.

'I hope Christ will make my death as easy as if I had died on a downy pillow,' he mockingly said to those in wait for his execution.

He hung for his atrocities at Ellis Island on April 22, 1831.

Afterwards, a museum in New York placed his skull on display, a testament to his punishment.

A Reward for the Return of Two Prisoners

Although Cofresí and Gibbs were not a part of the *'Golden Age of Piracy,'* the period between the 1650s and the 1730s when Captain Kidd and Blackbeard sailed, acts of robbery and mayhem still occurred around the Virgin Islands.

It's no surprise that silver dollars dating to this period could be found stashed away in a cave or buried on a beach.

The island of St. Thomas was a favorite resort for those daring marauders, partly because of its beautiful harbor and central location, and partly because of its natural convenience for careening and refitting their vessels.

In St. Thomas, a reward was offered of 200 pieces-of-eight for the capture of two prisoners accused of piracy. They made their escape and absconded from Fort Christian on the morning of August 20, 1825.

200 Pieces of Eight Reward !

IS hereby offered for the apprehension of a Mulatto Man named **WILLIAM LEE,** arrested and under prosecution for Piracy, and who made his escape from Prison this morning; or for such information as can lead to his apprehension.—All persons are further warned from harbouring the said Prisoner under penalty as the Law directs.

St. Thomas, Office of Police, 26th May, 1825.

N. GIELLERUP.

Their names were Cornelius Sutton, aged 37 years, and William Lee, aged 38 years.

Anyone who harbored them knew they would be punished with the utmost severity.

Both men were described as mulatto and natives of New York.

Sutton was tall, stout, and blind in one eye, which had sunken in over the years. Lee was described as about five feet in height, slender, marked with smallpox and freckled-faced. No word was ever given about their capture.

However, four months after this notice was published, two more men living on the island of St. Thomas were captured and hung for pursuing horrible crimes.

"Some convicts bore their sentence with a manly resolution and bravery, while others with dejection and timidity."

The Danish West Indies were actively suppressing piracy, and this was 'a warning to those who might have the misfortune to allow their unbridled passions or other ideas to violate the laws of society.'

Death by the gallows was the destiny that awaited them!

The local newspaper provided the following details about their execution. (*The Sanct Thomae Tidende*)

Fort Christian, built in 1671 in St. Thomas, Danish West Indies © Royal Danish Library

Two Hung for Horrid Atrocities ~ 1825

In September 1825, William Hellyer, a Caucasian man, and Phoenix Phyfer, a free colored man, were charged and convicted for horrid atrocities.

A detailed account of their felony was never published, only a summary of their last moments alive.

On the appointed day, the Minister of the Church of England escorted the prisoners along the narrow cobblestone stairwell to the rooftop terrace.

Reverend McLaughlin knew they were deeply pertinent for their crimes and consoled the men in their last moments.

He glanced down at their chained feet as they dragged against the brick pavers. The rattling sounds echoed off the musty walls and tugged at his heartstrings.

At the gallows, each man muttered his last prayer as tears of remorse fell from their faces.

The spectators felt for the unfortunate men, but everyone was satisfied with its justice and necessity. They shuddered at the recollection of the crimes for which both of them were atoning with their lives.

The crowd stood frozen in profound sadness, witnesses to the gruesome event. By 2 o'clock, the men were dead.

Members of the garrison removed their bodies and transported them by boat to their final burial place.

"Phyfer was a native of St. Thomas, from a respectable colored family. At an early age, he was sent to Scotland, where he was educated and taught the cabinet-making business.

"On his return, he followed his profession, and from his general good deportment, was respected by everyone in the community.

"Phyfer prospered in business, was married, and in fact, fortune seemed to smile upon him; until he purchased a small sloop and pursued the horrible crime for which they accused him.

"Hellyer, an accomplice with Phyfer, was a native of Portsmouth, England. He was 36 years of age and had commanded several merchant vessels with great regard.

He was survived by his wife and three children who lived in one of the Windward Islands."

The newspaper editor showed very little empathy towards the thieves.

"These lamentable men," he wrote, "while in possession of all that could render them happy (property and the esteem of everyone), deviated from the path of rectitude, and brought upon themselves a most deserved fate."

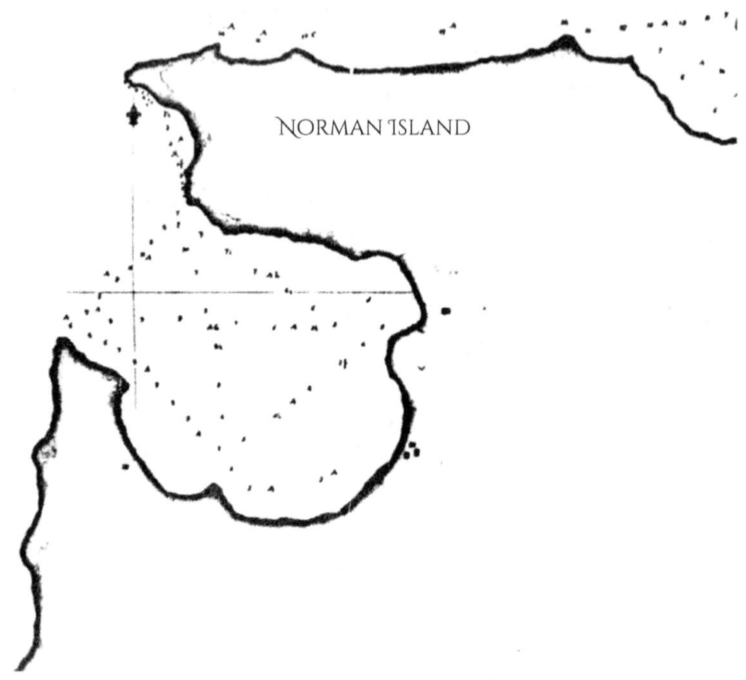

A Norman Island 'Pirate'

The British Virgin Islands were suffering the same torment.

In 1827, the *Sanct Thomae Tidende* carried the distressing intelligence of a crime of piracy committed at Norman Island.

IN conformity with superior orders, a Reward of

$ 300,

is hereby offered for the apprehension of

William Davies,

from the Island of Tortola, who has made himself guilty of piracy by taking possession of and carrying off a Vessel and its Cargo, which was laying at an anchor at Normands Island, and likewise $100 for the apprehension of every other person who has participated in said crime, which respective Sums will be paid as soon as one or more of said Persons are delivered in the Police Office.

Police Office, St. Thomas, 18th December, 1827.

PORTH,
Police Master pr: interim.

One William Davies became a wanted man for taking possession of a vessel laying at anchor and its cargo, making himself guilty as charged.

A large reward of $300 was placed on his head, and $100 was offered for the apprehension of his accomplices.

No further updates were ever given regarding Davies' eventual imprisonment.

The Truth About Finding Treasure

It's difficult to know the truth about the discovery of pirate treasure in one's family when all the parties involved have died, and no written record exists. We must rely on the oral stories passed down from one generation to another, and whatever documentary evidence one can find. Today, our family believes that:

Herman O. Creque
1884 - 1949

Henry Osmond Creque (1858-1915) shared the coins he found with his son, Herman Ogilvie Creque (1884-1949).

Herman then gifted several to his sons, Henry (1912-1957), and possibly Frank. (1915-1978)

During the mid-1950s, Henry (1912-1957) had nine of his silver dollars made into a necklace for Peggy.

Their children, William (Bill) Creque, and Juliette, both confirmed that the coins in their mother's necklace were found on Norman Island.

Bill believes it was Herman who first suggested to his sons that they have them made into jewelry as a gift for their wives.

Perhaps this is where *"The Legend of Norman Island"* first began, whereby a necklace of Spanish coins was given to every bride that married into the family.

1812 4-Real Coin ~ Joseph Napoleon Bonaparte

The Safe Deposit Box

If Herman gave his sons some of these precious coins, it raises the question, *What did he give to his three daughters, Olga, Valerie, and Margie?* Valerie, my grandmother, saved everything. Perhaps a clue to this mystery could be found in her safe deposit box.

One day when I peeked inside, I felt as though I was looking into Billy Bones' own sea chest!

Strewn along the interior of the box were golden Indian heads, King Christian Kroner, Liberty Head Double Eagles, Morgan Silver Dollars, as well as a 1972 Kennedy Half Dollar, which was intended as a memorial to the assassinated President of the United States.

The coins were from several countries and of different sizes. The diversity included English, French, Spanish, and Danish, representing some of the Kings and Queens of Europe for the last hundred years, as well as an equal amount of modern-day coinage from the US Mint.

There were even a few unique pieces, a 1979 Susan B. Anthony, the first time that a woman appeared on a U.S. circulating coin, and a 2001 Sacagawea Liberty Dollar with the image of a Native American female guide, Sacagawea, and her infant baby.

However, the early doubloons from the seventeenth and eighteenth century that I hoped to see, were not there. Instead, I found a Spanish coin that could have come from the same assortment that Henry received.

It was an 1812 four-real silver coin with the image of the King of Spain, Joseph Napoleon Bonaparte.

Joseph Bonaparte

I was excited to find that this coinage matched the type and date range for Peggy's necklace. This was interesting, and could establish a connection, but I needed more proof.

As time passed, I was convinced that Peggy had the answers I was looking for, but she remained reticent about sharing what she knew about Norman Island.

When I asked her again in 2013, specifically about the necklace that she received as a gift, she said, *"I don't know what you mean by the coin necklace."*

Two years later, I was still hoping she would tell me more, but I was disappointed when she responded with, *"I will have to try to dig back in my memory to help you with this."*

I knew she didn't want to discuss the matter, so I tried my best to be patient and understanding. Fortunately, a couple of years later, she seemed more receptive.

In 2015, she sent me an encouraging message.

> *"Val, dear, I am sorry I haven't answered your questions yet.*
> *I have been busy. I will try to help you tomorrow.*
> *I enjoy doing it. Love, Aunt Peggy"*

Peggy had been a member of our family for sixty years. When she finally addressed some of my inquires, I knew then I was about to discover a few family secrets.

Here are the tantalizing tales she told me about Norman Island, some believable—and some out of this world! You can decide for yourself... *Fact or fiction?*

Henry Ogilvie Creque, 1912 - 1957

Meeting Councilman Creque

Peggy confided that she first arrived on the island of St. Thomas in November 1952 and stayed at the iconic Bluebeard's Castle, which overlooked the harbor and beautiful town.

One evening, while she was enjoying a drink on the terrace, Munroe Trotman, who was a popular bartender, approached her.

He pointed to a man in a white suit sitting at the bar alone and told her that the gentleman wanted to meet her.

Peggy nodded, and Munroe escorted Henry over to her table and introduced him.

"Madam, permit me to acquaint you with Councilman Henry O. Creque."

Henry likely bent to kiss her hand. He was charming and had a natural gift for mesmerizing his female audiences, captivating them with his magnetic personality.

From the very moment they met, Peggy said, their romance blossomed, and they became inseparable.

Two months later, they were married. (January 3, 1953)

*1950s
Campaign Pin*

Prior to meeting Peggy, Henry was a senator, like his father before him, and represented the island of St. Thomas as a member of the Colonial Council.

His Chevrolet Dealership kept him busy, and yet, since his father's death in 1949, he was also responsible for the daily operations of the Creque Marine Railway on Hassel Island.

The Creque Marine Railway

The facility was the oldest steam-powered railway in the Western Hemisphere and the only dockyard in the Caribbean large enough to take ships up to twelve hundred tons.

Henry's grandfather purchased the 11-acre property in 1910 and refurbished the rails before its grand opening in 1912.

On one occasion, while Henry was at Hassel Island, Peggy said that a notable sailor brought his vessel in for repairs. Kit S. Kapp (1926-2013) was the captain and owner of the 50-foot ketch *Fairwinds,* along with his wife, Valerie.

The couple were early pioneers in the yacht charter industry that flourished in the Virgin Islands during the 1950s.

As Captain Kapp and Henry were getting acquainted one day, the conversation turned to pirates and hidden treasure.

The schooner, Venture on the rails at the Creque Marine Railway ~ 1912

According to Capt. Kapp, whom I spoke to by telephone in 1996, Henry retrieved an ancient object from his office on the slip and presented it to him for viewing.

It was a small sword, rusty in parts, but the hilt was encrusted with small gemstones.

Kapp remembered it had a curved blade, possibly 22 to 24 inches, and reminded him of a Civil War relic. He added, '*It couldn't have come from the sea, as it would have long disintegrated.*'

When Kapp questioned Henry about its origins, he told him, '*My grandfather found it on Norman Island.*'

Unfortunately, no one in the family alive today was aware of its existence or what may have happened to the relic, but another visitor to the railway shared a similar experience.

Harry and his wife, Jeanne Perkins Harman, owned *The Love Junk*, a forty-foot Navy barge they converted to a glass-bottom boat. They took tourists out on excursions around the harbor during the 1940s.

Every few months, the boat needed to be hauled so that the bottom could be scraped free of its barnacles, and a fresh coat of paint added. Since the boatyard was across the channel from their dock, Mrs. Harmon wanted to visit and meet Henry. She had heard so much about him from her husband.

According to her novel, *The Love Junk*, before Jeanne arrived, she contacted Henry to let him know of her upcoming visit.

Henry O. Creque
1912 - 1957

Henry agreed to let her come over, but first, he had to telephone the yard and warn the crew.

"Tell the boys to get their clothes on, Watchie," he said. *"Mistress Harman is coming over."*

"The crew," Henry explained, "were six strapping young bucks straight out of Tortola that habitually worked stark naked, except for shoes and straw hats."

The Watchman,
nicknamed, Watchie

As Jeanne strolled around the dry-dock, she couldn't believe how beautiful the surroundings were. She wrote:

"The tropical jungle that curled around the water's edge included royal palms, lantanas, and banana trees laden with golden fruit. They crowded against each other in a race to cover the paved cobblestones."

"The air was heavy, she noticed, with the fragrance of bay leaves, ripe papayas, pink mangoes, and the blossom of every conceivable island flower."

"They blended in a riot of color ranging from the delicate, blue, white of the tree orchids to the rich, sensually formed, flaming-red hibiscus."

The Creque Marine Railway © Creque Family Archives

"Dominating the lush scene was an exquisite old stone house, one of the island's fine pieces of Danish architecture.

The archways framing the doors were of faded pink granite, brought over from Scotland as ballast by the ships calling for West Indian sugar and rum."

While meandering along the pathways, admiring the enormous old anchors tossed here and there, Henry confessed, '*My grandfather built the yard with some of the treasure he found on Norman Island.*'

This was an incredible revelation, which she quickly jotted down in her notebook.

On a subsequent visit to Tortola, Jeanne Harmon wrote, '*Natives of Tortola confirmed to her that Henry's grandfather had discovered over a million dollars' worth of treasure there, hidden away on a ledge, deep inside a cave filled with bats.*'

A Family Secret

I was thrilled when Aunt Peggy finally agreed to share a family secret! At last, I would know the origins of my ancestor's wealth and the untold story everyone was reluctant to share.

Peggy conceded that the story about her late husband's grandfather finding treasure in the British Virgin Islands was true, and that it could be verified in a book that was published years prior.

'*It was the reason the Creque's came to St. Thomas,*' she added.

The book she spoke of was entitled "*The Golden Parrot.*"

Excited by this encouraging news, I rushed to find a copy locally, but unfortunately, it was no longer in print. Thankfully, the Library of Congress mailed me a duplicate photocopy.

The Golden Parrot was a fascinating treasure tale about the discovery of buried treasure on Norman Island.

Frederic A. Fenger, an American yacht designer and avid sailor, published the manuscript in 1921. He toured the Virgin Islands and the West Indies alone on a seventeen-foot canoe he designed. The *Yakaboo*, as he called it, was an expression used by islanders in the Pacific, which meant, *Goodbye*.

After perusing the novel, it was apparent that Fenger knew of H.O. Creque and something of the treasure found in the British Virgins.

However, I was disappointed to learn that he distrusted him, and painted him as the antagonist in his story, referring to him as, "*The dirtiest scoundrel this side of Haiti.*"

Although, his references to Henry in his Pongee suit and Pith helmet rang true, the derogatory sentiments about his character did not.

Chapter 2

Frederic Fenger's Treasure Tale 1921

Frederic A. Fenger on the Yakaboo

Alone in the Caribbean ~ 1917

Frederic A. Fenger first visited the island of St. Thomas in 1911, and then again in 1914, and 1915, when the island formed part of the Danish West Indies.

On Fenger's first voyage to the Caribbean, he paddled and sailed through the islands and shared those adventures in his first book, *Alone in the Caribbean,* published in 1917.

Below is his brief account of his first tour of the British Virgin Islands.

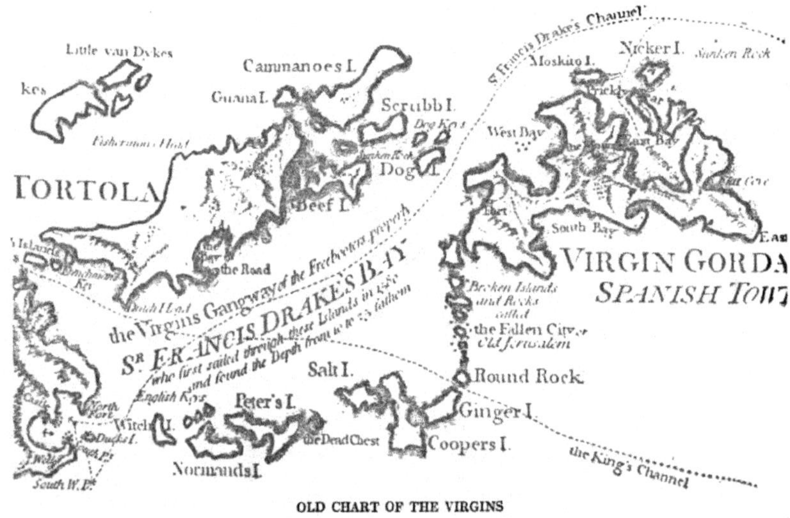

OLD CHART OF THE VIRGINS

Visiting Tortola

"It was Thursday, June 22nd, 1911, he wrote, the Coronation Day of George the Fifth, when my little sailing canoe anchored in the pretty harbour of Tortola, having arrived from visiting Saba Island in the Dutch Antilles.

Government House ~ Tortola, British Virgin Islands © The Sheen Collection

I was no stranger to the West Indies and went ashore to announce my arrival. I was welcomed warmly by the Commissioner, Leslie Jarvis.

From the verandah at Government House, I marveled at the view, taking in Salt, Cooper, and Ginger islands across the channel.

When I expressed a desire to visit them, the Commissioner agreed to drop me off at Virgin Gorda. From there, I could paddle through the islands, visiting them one by one.

The next morning, after an enjoyable breakfast, the group embarked on a trip to several of the islands in commemoration of the King's Coronation.

Special treats of pineapple syrup, baskets of buns, and boxes of Coronation medals for each school child were going to be disbursed.

Lady Constance © The National Archives

The Cutter, Lady Constance

The government's sailing cutter, *Lady Constance,* was loaded for the trip. Besides the goodies, there were guns, rods, and a leather case with the Governor's official helmet.

Our first stop was East End.

We shared the treats and commemorative medals with the fortunate recipients, then set a course for Virgin Gorda.

From there, I disembarked with my canoe and sailed out through the narrow passage by Mosquito Island.

I was eager to explore the out-islands on my own.

Mosquito Island was first granted to Edward Coakley on June 2, 1724, by Governor John Hart.

Virgin Gorda

On Virgin Gorda, I was surprised to find no town, merely clusters of native huts. The two larger settlements had small schoolhouses, which I noticed were also used as churches.

Life in these small outer cays was very simple. One lived by raising a few ground provisions near his hut and when he wished to change his diet, he went fishing.

To get cash, he sent his fish and ground provisions to the market in Tortola or St. Thomas. Strange to say, his most urgent need for cash was for the purchase of tobacco.

Fenger shared an interesting story of what happened when the island ran out of this important necessity. It was during the hurricane season when all the sloops were at St. Thomas.

They were gone about a week, he said, and were due to return when suspicious weather set in, and they could not leave St. Thomas.

Once two days passed with no tobacco, he found the residents reverting to drastic measures for a smoke.

They dried leaves of various bushes and tried to smoke them with little success. They next burned dried grass and small pieces of bone. Those hard pressed took to pulling the oakum out of the seams of an old boat that lay on the beach.

At last, the threat of a hurricane passed, and the home-bound sloops were sighted! As soon as the boats were beached, the first business of the island was to enjoy a good smoke!

He watched in amazement as two hundred columns of bluish smoke drifted up in the light easterly breeze!

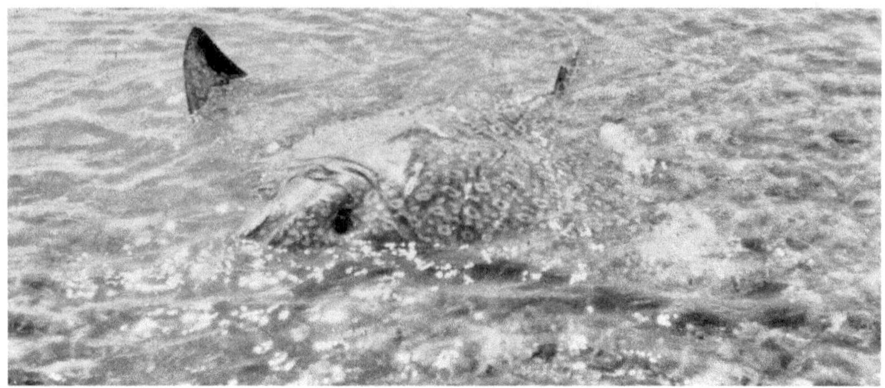

Devil Fish © Creque Family Archives

Ginger Island

In the morning, Fenger was sailing towards Ginger Island when he spotted a huge devil fish.

His fin, mottled brown and black like the rest of his upper surface, stood nearly three feet high! He judged its size to be about eighteen feet across from tip to tip.

Cooper Island

Having given the animal a wide berth, he landed at the little beach on Cooper Island, an island of about forty acres. There, Fenger stopped to mend his mainsail, where a batten had worn through its pocket.

It was a great joy for him to be able to do a bit of beach work. He sat for a while under the small trees where the cool wind seeped through the shade. When he finished, he shoved off again.

The Governor of the Leeward Islands, William Matthew, first granted the island to Philip Markoe on February 19, 1730. Markoe was a trusted friend of Francis Crequi, my 9x great-grandfather.

Salt Island © Thomas Dixon Green

Salt Island

Fenger went ashore on the beach at Salt Island where a few huts flocked together under the coco-palms. There, he met an interesting resident, William Penn.

Becoming friends after a few exchanges, William told the captain about the history of the island and the sinking of the Royal Mail Steamer, *RMS Rhone* that wrecked in the hurricane.

As proof, he showed him a gilded mirror which had been '*dove up*' from the sea floor. Intrigued, they both visited the site briefly, before the captain said goodbye and sailed for his next destination.

Peter Island

Fenger stopped next at Peter Island, which rose about five hundred feet from the sea and was twice as large as its neighbor, Norman Island.

Peter Island © Frederic A. Fenger

He settled there for the night and pitched his tent on the beach. Within moments, the wind suddenly dropped and *out of the bush came thousands of mosquitoes on a rampage!*

As they attacked him, he started beating the air frantically with a towel! Finally, when a gentle breeze sprang up, he could settle down and get some sleep.

His final destination was Norman Island –… where a treasure had been found. There was a tree on the island with certain cabalistic marks, he said, which were supposed to indicate the presence of buried treasure.

Fenger then cleared the end of Pelican Cay and hauled up for the Bight. Norman Island is long and narrow, with an arm that runs westward from its northern shore, forming a deep harbour.

"It offered excellent protection from all quarters but northeast."

Norman Island © Frederic A. Fenger

Norman Island and the Treasure Caves

"In a rocky wall on the extreme western end of the island, where the harbour opened out to the channel, were three caves which could be easily seen when sailing through the Flanagan passage into the Sir Francis Drake Channel.

"These caves are the ordinary deep hollows one commonly finds in volcanic rock formations," he wrote, "close to the sea, and were for years, unsuspected of holding hidden treasure."

Fenger reported that "a certain Black merchant of St. Thomas, who had literally become rich overnight, found his money in the shape of Spanish doubloons from an iron chest which he dug up in the far end of one cave."

"The man had bought Norman Island, had spent some time there, and for no apparent reason, had suddenly become rich.

One day, a curious fisherman found an empty chest by the freshly dug hole in the cave and there were even a few telltale coins that had rolled out of range of the lantern of the man who dug out the treasure.

And there must have been another place, because one day, a small schooner came down from the north."

"She entered at the port of Road Town and picked up a native from Salt Island, and one night, she ran down to Norman's."

"The next morning, she put the native ashore on his own island and sailed for parts unknown. As to what happened on Norman," he said, "the native, it seems, was strangely silent."

The Beach in the Bight

"When Fenger sailed into the harbour, he saw a sandy beach at the far end, where a small wooden jetty stood out in the calm water. Fringing the beach was a row of small coco palms, behind which the island bowled up into a sort of amphitheater of scrubby hillside.

What a place for a pirate's nest!

There is scant printed history of Norman and what is written is mostly in some such records as led the schooner to the island.

He rowed in towards the beach, the hill to the eastward cutting off all moving air so that a calm of deathly stillness held the head of the bay in a state of quivering heat waves.

The low burr of wind in the upper air out-voiced whatever sound might have come from the surf on the windward side of the island.

There was something peculiarly uncanny about the place, which was even more accentuated by the lonely jetty.

There was a pair of pelicans that launched forth from their perch on the gallows-like frame at its end.

They flew off as he tied up to the jetty but completed their circle as he stepped ashore and sat eyeing the *Yakaboo,* as if detailed there on sentry duty."

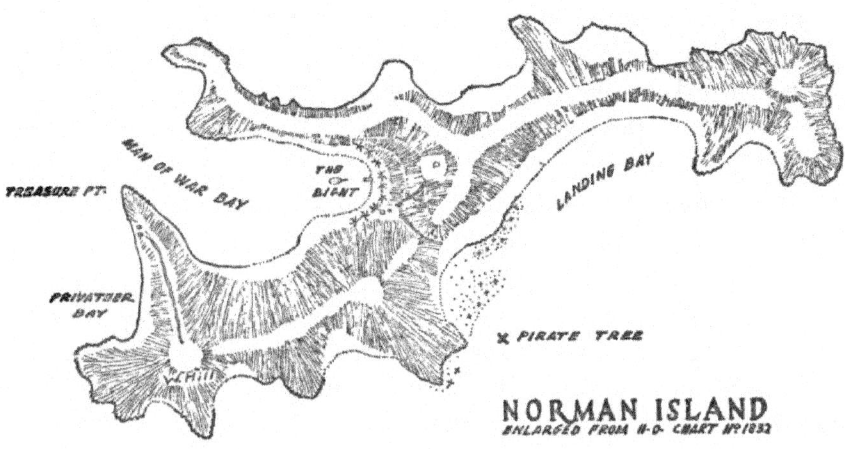

"The heat was intolerable and if he were to camp on Norman, he would have to find a cooler spot.

First, however, he would hunt for the pirate tree. It was northeast of the jetty, in a grove which mounts the ridge, but he had not gone far into the bush before he began to feel faint and sick.

The bush was close, but shaded, and as he retraced his steps to the jetty and came out again into the full glare of the beach, the heat came upon him like a blow.

He needed water, and he knew where he could get it, lukewarm, in his can in the after-compartment of the canoe.

He tried to stoop down from the jetty but nearly fell off, so he followed the safer plan of lying down on the burning boards and reaching into the compartment with his arms and head hanging over.

Shooting Two Nuts in the Neck

If he could only get one of those coconuts, he should feel much better, and although the trees were young and the nuts hung low, they were still nearly three feet above his reach."

"Perhaps he could shoot them down, so he went back to the canoe and got the rifle, which so far had been of little use to him. The will of the good Lord was with him, for he found that he could almost touch the nuts with the muzzle of his rifle.

By resting the barrel upward along the trunk of the tree, he could poke the muzzle within a few inches of the stems."

Anyone could have made the shot, but he missed because he forgot that the sight was raised a good half inch from the center of the bore. It took him some time to reason this out, and he had to sit down for a while to recover from the shock of the recoil.

Then an idea came to him!

He aimed the rifle, this time with its axis in line with the stem and pulled the trigger. Down came the nut, and he blew off its head and drank its cool liquid.

In like manner, he shot another coconut. Stalking the fruit of a coco palm may sound like the keenest of sports, but no hunting ever gave him keener satisfaction than shooting these two nuts in the neck.

The milk was cool and refreshing and he believed that it pulled him out of as tight a corner as he had ever been in alone. There was no one living on the island to help him.

The coming on of nausea and the feeling that he did not exactly care what happened was hideous to his better sense, and he felt that at all costs, he must try to refresh himself and then leave the island as soon as possible.

By sheer luck of super caution, he got into the canoe and untied the painter, and then in one last effort of fostered strength, he rowed out of the cove into the breeze where he quietly pulled in his oars and lay down."

A little time later, the quick roll of the canoe roused him, and he found he was clear of Norman and close upon Flanagan Island. The wind was cool, and he made sail for Tortola.

He was still very faint, but he had held that mainsheet for so many miles that even half insensible, he could sail the *Yakaboo* into Road Harbour without looking.

Norman Island can be an inhospitable island if you're not prepared.

The Golden Parrot ~ 1921

Fenger's second publication was entitled *The Golden Parrot,* the story I was so eager to read.

One of the main characters was a man named Old Tompas, an unreputable, Mulatto merchant who owned a ship chandlery business in St. Thomas.

Fenger imbued him with many of the physical attributes that H.O. Creque possessed, but painted him as an unsavory character, *"full of dirty tricks."*

He left very little doubt who Old Tompas was modeled after and wrote…

"Around the corner from the dock stood the cook, talking with a gaunt mulatto of about sixty in a Pongee suit and Pith helmet.

The two were apparently engrossed in earnest conversation, for as the artist and the broker watched, the cook eased the bundles in his arms as if to gather more clearly the import of what the other was saying.

Carrahua! It's that dyad Tompas! and grabbing the artist by the arm, the broker drew him back."

"That Old Tompas is the dirtiest scoundrel this side of Haiti and he's a dyam good man to keep your cook away from."

"Yes, but what could he do?"

"The words came with unpleasant familiarity and Richard could hardly conceal all trace of anxiety as he added, We'll only be here a few days."

"Old Tompas has the only small dock between Barbados and Cuba, took up the broker, "and if he can get you up there, it'll cost you dear before you get down again."

"If your cook is in cahoots with him," Fenger continued, "kerosene isn't the only way to make a bilge leak; or a cut lanyard might let your mast go as soon as you get out in the breeze. "

"He's got the only spars in St. Thomas, and he knows it. The broker seemed to be quoting from experience."

"He's full of dirty tricks."

"What did you say his name was?" asked Richard, "by way of turning the conversation back into local channels."

The St. Thomas harbor is full of ships, Danish West Indies

"Tompas – we've called him *Old Tompas* ever since his father died. My uncle used to tell how the *Old Tompas* – the grandfather of this one got his start in business."

"Way back in the twenties, (1820s) when the harbor was so full of ships, you could almost jump across from one to another. The *Old Tompas* kept a sailor's boarding house and was his own runner."

Spanish Gold Buried on the Island

"In those days, there lived an old hermit on one of the islands east of here. In some way, Tompas learned that the hermit knew where there was Spanish gold buried on the island."

"At the mention of the hermit and the treasure, the lads' hearts leaped within them, but they betrayed no outward sign," and the broker continued:

"Tompas went to the island one night and he must have forced the hermit to tell him where the treasure was hidden – at any rate, he sold out his crimping business one day and bought a trading schooner, and after a while, he bought more until he had a small fleet of them."

Richard looked across at the artist as if to say, "That must have been a mere dollop he left in the cave to avert suspicion."

"But what became of the hermit?" Pursued the artist.

"Oh, he died in time and then Tompas bought the island – said he was going to raise sheep on it; but he never bothered about the sheep. When he died, it passed on to his son, and then this Tompas kept it for a while, but he sold it at last to a man in Tortola."

"The people said he let it go because he didn't find what he was looking for."

"And what island did you say this Tompas owned?"

"It's called Norman Island, one of the British cays to the east of here – I've never been there, but my uncle used to speak of it.

They say there's an old tree on it with pirate marks on the trunk. But no one has ever been able to make 'em out, and if anyone had, he wouldn't have told.

The natives used to go over there and dig all around the tree till at last, the Commissioner had to put a stop to it.

When a native once got the fever, it spoiled him for work. It got so bad once that the cotton nearly went to pot, and the price of fish went sky high."

A Cave with Doubloons

"They say the Old Tompas got his doubloons from a cave in another part of the island and that this Tompas believed for a long time there was treasure to be found on the island – somewhere."

"The queer part of it is that this cave is one of three that opened right on the channel in plain sight of everyone who sails by, and there it had been lying for no one knows how many years.

But I wouldn't waste a dyam hour on the island, for there have been enough people over there for the last ninety years to dig up the whole of it.

Carrahua! I'd like to get my fingers under the old devil's hide, said the broker.

I once had a Nova Scotiaman come in here cosigned to me and she was leaking badly."

The Creque Marine Railway, Hassel Island

"We unloaded her cargo in the old devil's warehouse and hauled her out on his ways for caulking.

And when she got off, she leaked as bad as ever.

Then Old Tompas spread the word that she was unseaworthy and wouldn't hold her caulking.

You see, he wanted to have her condemned so that he could buy her himself.

Her Bluenose skipper made a great fuss, so we hauled her out again and found that she was as sound as a nut ~

Someone had opened a couple of seams the night before she got off the first time.

We couldn't prove anything against Tompas, and we had to pay him for two hauling's to boot.

The old robber had her cargo, you see. The owners got rid of the captain, honest old man he was, too, and they took their trade away from me!"

"There was an evil sound to that name Tompas, and the lads began to feel that they were being drawn into something more than a mere adventure."

A Description of 'Old Tompas'

"For the first time, the lad got a good view of the Mulatto's face. Except for the color of the skin, which was indeed almost light enough to that of a Spaniard, there was little to suggest the African but for the rather full curves of an almost cosmopolitan countenance."

Henry O. Creque
1858 – 1915
Born: Anegada
Died: St.. Thomas

"Had the artist known, he might have traced something of the old French blood from the white days of Haiti, woven with the Spanish of Santo Domingo through the negro of the Virgins."

"Soon, a small sloop was making out from the wharf, behind which was a yellow building where he read the words," *'O.V. Tompas – Ship's Supplies – American Lumber.'"*

Interestingly, similar signage was found on H.O. Creque's Warehouse, *H.O. Creque – Ship's Supplies – American Lumber.*

Fenger's Own Treasure Hunt

Intrigued by the thought of finding pirate gold, Fenger set out on his own treasure hunt with William Penn, whom he befriended on Peter Island.

When he heard Penn's story about his grandfather living on Norman Island, and that he knew where the old hermit's house was located, hasty plans were thrown together to have a look.

Despite knowing that 'Old Tompas' owned the island; nothing would keep him from the possibility of finding hidden riches.

Perhaps Fenger's account was just a good ole yarn, but there were elements of truth interwoven into his chapters.

Hunting for the Hermit's House

"When Penn took them to the location where his grandfather may have lived, the trees began to thin and presently the four came out upon an open plateau, a scant acre in extent lying under the brow of the hill."

"Penn halted a moment to get his bearings and then made for the center of the clearing. Drawing near, they made out a rectangular patch in the scrub grass, which resolved itself into a low wall of masonry scarcely a foot high, some thirty feet square. It was formed of rough blocks of coral rock cemented together."

"This is the foundation of the old hermit's house," Penn said.

"Plenty people been digging round here, he chuckled, but de ol hermit, he cute, he know better dan plant money *inside* de house."

"Fishing out the compass, the foundations lay to the cardinal points. Placing the compass on the southwest corner, the lads sighted a line directly southwest along which they measured off six fathoms. At this point, they laid off a square of some six feet, and here began to dig.

The ground was loose and loamy, admirably adapted for a garden and it was not long before the native had cleared a hole knee deep.

The hole was now almost waist deep. The earth had sunk away a few inches in one corner and here Penn was excitedly burrowing with his hands."

"Oh, my fadder, wot is dis?"

"He held up a lump of something in one hand while still digging with the other. It was a crumbling piece of rotted wood.

Then, sitting up on his haunches, he rubbed something on the ridge of his thigh and held it up to the lads who were bending over him.

It was round and shining, and yellow, and showed the austere features of Carlos IV, Hisp. & Ind. R. It bore the date, 1771.

Penn cleared the earth from a hole into which he had thrust his hand. There were more pieces of crumbling wood and the hole widened to a circle of metal some two feet in diameter.

It was the rim of an iron pot, such as was used in the old days for boiling soap, filled nearly to the top with earth-stained discs.

Again, he reached down with both hands and dumped a load of clinking doubloons on the grass by the knees of the lads. Nothing but doubloons!"

"What a find!" exclaimed Richard.

"How are we going to get them all down to the schooner? The resourceful Gus had already thought of it and jumping out of the pit, he began to remove his trousers. Then he knotted the ends and began scooping the doubloons into the twin bags.

When they were about half full, he stood up and hoisted them to his shoulder, slinging the legs fore and aft. I never thought they would weigh so much; I must have all of sixty pounds!

They estimated afterwards that they must have some two hundred and sixty pounds, sixty-eight thousand dollars, a tidy enough sum."

The Golden Parrot © Frederic A. Fenger

"This, of course, was not the sixty thousand pounds sterling mentioned by Captain Southey (See Chapter 5), nor would old Norman have left such a miserly amount. That is why from the very first, Fenger maintained that what the tads found was only a part of a worthless cache left by some upstart privateer of a later day.

And now, he says, four shirt-tailed adventurers are trudging barelegged on their way to the beach with pants full of doubloons!"

The First Published Account about Treasure

Despite Fenger's strong dislike for H.O. Creque and the unsavory way he portrayed his character in his books, the indirect references about Henry's discovery of treasure in the British Virgins were the first published accounts, as early as 1917, that acknowledged the rumours and their possible validity.

However, almost one hundred and fifty years prior, a much larger treasure cache had been discovered on Norman Island.

Unlike Henry's reported find in a cave, this concealment was well documented in the archival records in Europe, America, and the Caribbean.

Chapter 3

Searching for Spanish Treasure
1750

The history of Norman Island is rooted in piracy and it's no surprise that one of the most remarkable discoveries of stolen treasure in the world was made on the tiny isle over two hundred and seventy years ago.

Fifty chests with 150,000 pieces-of-eight, decorative silver, cochineal, indigo, and tobacco were brought to a bay at Norman Island, where a large quantity of the silver was secreted away.

On November 4, 1750, *'the inhabitants of Tortola got wind of it, found it and dug it up, then shared it amongst themselves as a lawful prize.'*

This sparked an international manhunt to find and arrest the pirates responsible for the crime, and those who later dug it up.

Many biographers, who write about the life of pirates, profess that buccaneers rarely buried any treasure, but instead, spent their rewards on simple pleasures like liquor, women, and gambling, but this true story disproves that theory.

The Treasure's Value

In today's value, the stolen treasure would be worth in the multiple millions of dollars, especially since the story surrounding its theft was well documented in the archives.

Successful treasure hunters, Mel Fisher, Barry Clifford, and Burt Webber discovered great riches from sunken treasure ships, but the treasure on Norman Island was one of very few hidden caches, perhaps only a handful, ever discovered on a Caribbean Island.

The following account documents the sad misfortune, and ultimate betrayal that preceded this remarkable discovery.

La Nuestra Señora de Guadalupe and her Ill-Fated Fleet

A Seventeenth Century Spanish Galleon

The year was 1750.

The Spanish Galleon, *La Nuestra Señora de Guadalupe*, one of seven in the flotilla, departed Havana, Cuba, with a valuable cargo of Mexican silver, milled from the mines at Veracruz.

Her convoy sailed under the direction of the guardian flagship, *La Galga*, a Man-of-War bound for Cadiz, Spain. She was their protector, the most heavily armed ship in the fleet.

Sailing in the convoy aboard her sister ship, *La Nuestra Señora de Los Godos*, was the Governor of Havana, one of the most esteemed passengers with a valuable fortune stored in the hold.

Had it not been for that doomful decision to head out to sea on August 18, 1750, when the Atlantic hurricane season was most active, there would be no tale to tell….no great discovery of silver dollars or church plate glistening in the sand on a secluded beach.

Most of the following account came from the captain himself, Don Juan Manuel Bonilla as he reflected on the tormented experience he had, trying to save his ship, its passengers, and the valuable cargo entrusted to him.

The whole affair almost cost him his life!

Setting Sail for Spain

It was a beautiful day around noon when all the ships happily passed through the *Old Bahama Channel* together, before the cloud formations darkened and the weather deteriorated.

What Bonilla thought was a light rain, quickly turned into heavy thunder gusts. Before long, the constant deluge of a very great storm scattered the ships over a wide area.

The more experienced sailors grew concerned when the vessel started to sway, pushed uncontrollably by the invisible force.

At three in the afternoon, the wind hit them from the north with such great strength. It raged on without ceasing for days until the storm strengthened into a devastating hurricane.

The frightened passengers clasped their rosaries and prayed vociferously to *Saint Medardus*.

He was the patron saint for the protection from storms, but hours passed and there was still no answer to their pleas.

Saint Medardus

The wind howled and whistled as it squeezed through the cracks near the portholes, like a ghost, penetrating their shivering bodies with salted sea spray.

Cold, seasick, and consumed with fear, they regretted their departure.

Sadly, their ship could offer no comfort, despite being named in honor of the Blessed Virgin Mary.

Saving the Storm-Damaged Ship

The crew did their utmost and worked all four pumps continuously trying to keep the ship from flooding, but they could not keep up.

The rudder snapped and was lost, and when the lashing by the wind grew more intense, the masts and the riggings snapped too.

With a heavy thud, they landed on the deck, shaking the entire ship and the terrified travelers to exhaustion.

According to *Treasure Island: The Untold Story*, the passengers endured five days of terror as they were driven further and further from their intended destination.

The fleet was now northeast of Cape Canaveral, Florida being pushed northwards towards the Carolinas.

Just when they thought all was lost, the winds lightened a bit, and a ray of hope eased their fears. The high seas had forced them along *a wild and lonely coast,* somewhere near Cape Hatteras.

There, they took shelter until they could proceed to Ocracoke Inlet five leagues away. They hoped to find a skillful pilot to bring them over the sandbar and closer to shore for safety.

A Mutiny Over Money

Given the deplorable condition the vessel was in, they were lucky to have made it to Ocracoke. Once there, Bonilla became concerned about the cargo.

He purchased a packet boat as soon as he could and ordered all the chests of silver brought on shore for protection, but as he did so, he had no idea that the crew were secretly plotting to plunder his ship!

Over the next two days, the sailors laboriously transported about fifty heavy chests to the beach, but one mate by the name of Pedro Rodriguez saw an opportunity to abandon his duty and encouraged the other sailors to join him.

To stop the impending mutiny, Bonilla promised to give them double their wages as soon as the cargo was safe.

However, the crew demanded to be paid *immediately*, since they could see that there was enough silver on shore to do it, insisting that they fulfilled their duties, and their contract was over.

Otherwise, they refused to work the pumps to keep the ship afloat.

With no way to remedy the situation, Bonilla offered to pay the men, but they demanded 100 dollars each!

Eventually, he conceded, but not before he made them complete their task of moving all the silver and the bags of cochineal ashore.

Cochineal, a red dye used for tinting fabrics, was made from the bodies of little dried bugs. It was second only to silver as Spain's most valuable New World commodity.

Nowhere in the world was so successful at harvesting this tiny valuable bug!

Robbing the Passengers of Jewels

Once the task was accomplished, some seamen took advantage of the situation and broke open the passengers' trunks and robbed them of their jewels and other valuables.

They were angry and committed such outrageous crimes that Bonilla chose rather to *pass in silence,* than to trouble His Excellency with the distressing news.

The passengers complained, but despite their cries, Bonilla felt he could not prevail on the seamen by any means to return the goods to their right owners.

He had lost control.

He watched helplessly as the crew behaved themselves in a most horrific manner, like indigent, desperate outlaws encouraged by Pedro Rodriquez, who acted like a crazy man.

Guarding the Galleon

Bonilla knew he needed urgent help and penned a letter to the Chief Pilot for help from the Captain General of Virginia.

Then, he hurriedly wrote a letter to Daniel Huony, the Captain of His Majesty's Ship, *La Galga,* to apprise him of the ominous situation.

Time was running out, but Bonilla was unsure of his next move since so many days had elapsed without knowing if anyone would come to his aid.

Remembering how far away he was, and that the silver on shore was not well guarded, he thought it best to transport the cargo to Virginia himself, but there was more to fear than he realized.

The Fear of Running Aground

With continuous storms still blowing hard on the coast and the bay being very shallow, Bonilla could sense his luck going from bad to worse.

After surviving the most dreadful experience of his life and having put forth all his effort to save his ship, he seemed destined to lose it in what he thought was a protected harbor.

Unfortunately, the tide was unstable and with every ebb and flow, the creaking planks voiced their anger, moaning and crackling under the pressure of insufficient water.

Afraid of the continuous blows and what might give way, Bonilla thought it best to call all the officers together for an urgent meeting. Seeing nothing but danger all around him, he decided not to wait any longer. He hired two available sloops to transport the most valuable portion of the cargo to Virginia. From there, it would be easy to find passage to Spain. There was no time to waste.

An Offer of Help Arrives

When one of the vessels was fully loaded and the other had the greatest part of her cargo on board, an officer of importance finally arrived, sent by the Captain General himself.

With him was a letter expressing *the good zeal and desire* the Captain General had to see Bonilla's cargo in a place of safety.

Since it was exposed on the coast and vulnerable, he offered to send him a sloop-of-war to transport the silver and cochineal to a guarded facility.

Bonilla was grateful, but since he had heard nothing for so long, he thought it best to accompany the officer to see the Captain General.

Loading the Chests of Coins

He wanted to consult with him about the best way to save the cargo under his charge. He said he took this step as *the most convenient way* to effect it, but it was a pivotal moment that would change the course of history and cost him dearly.

The visiting officer ordered the loading of the sloops halted until further orders were given.

In the meantime, Bonilla placed ten guards on each vessel and provided written instructions for them to carry their sails on shore and to do everything else in his temporary absence to prevent the Englishmen from slipping their cables and sneaking away with it.

Placed aboard the *Seaflower,* that would eventually make its way to Norman Island, were 55 chests of coined silver and a considerable quantity of cochineal, tobacco, hides and decoratively worked silver. Aboard her sister sloop, the *Mary,* were approximately 54 chests of pieces-of-eight and a small box of valuable jewels.

Loading the chests of coins

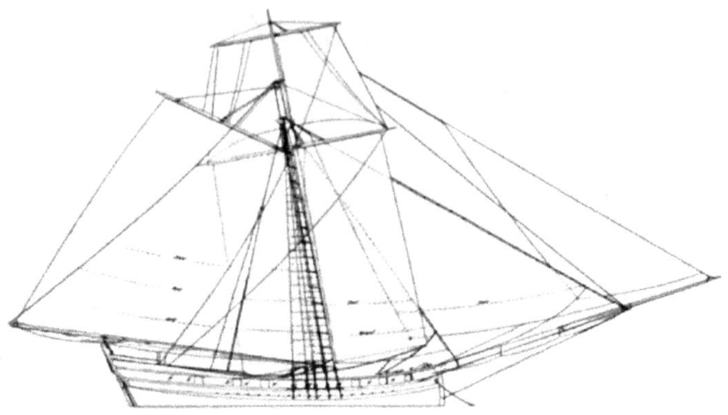

Virginia Sloop -1741, Drawn by H. I. Chapelle: Admiralty Records

An Opportunity to Flee with a Fortune

On the fourth day of Bonilla's absence, which was on the ninth of October, the restless Englishmen could wait no longer. The knowledge that 150,000 Spanish dollars lay tucked safely below in the hold tormented them.

With the wind blowing *fresh and fair*, both sloops seized an opportunity to flee. They clandestinely cut the cables to the *Guadalupe* around noon and crisscrossed their way to the open ocean.

Their vessels were light and built to fly, but fortunately for Bonilla, one of them ran aground on the sandbar and was caught by a pinnace full of people in desperate pursuit.

When Bonilla heard the dreadful news, it almost '*deprived him of his life and put him in a very weak state of health.'*

Despite the great care and diligence he took to secure the cargo, he could not believe the disobedience of the mate to whom he gave his explicit instructions. Against his orders, Rodriquez failed to remove the sloops' sails, nor did he keep a proper guard onboard of the vessels.

How could such a thing happen? This was his last instruction to the sailor!

It's uncertain why Bonilla trusted Rodriquez after the uprising and injurious influence he had over the crew. Perhaps Bonilla was partly responsible for the turn of events that led to his enormous loss.

Hunting for the Pirates

In a desperate panic, Bonilla made his applications to the Captain General and begged him to dispatch two vessels, one to the south coast, and the other to the north side, to search all the ports and creeks to find the culprits. They dispatched urgent expresses by land with the same precautions.

> *"I am in great trouble until I know the result of this. It is such a confusion. I endeavor to do my duty and take the proper steps in so intricate an affair, which I shall never forget."*

Bonilla was determined to search every coast from Ocracoke to the Dutch Island of Curaçao, St. Eustacia and the Danish Island of St. Thomas to find the felons. He did not know the extent it would take to locate the criminals and how much or how little he would get back of his precious cargo.

The Remaining Treasure

The Captain General finally sent the *Scorpion,* an English sloop-of-war, for the remaining shipment bound for Old Spain.

Included on the register were 50 chests of coined silver. Packed tightly into each chest were three bags with 1000 dollars each, along with two crates of worked silver, one small chest with precious jewels, 12 silver plates with the matching spoons and forks, and 134 bales of cochineal. Bonilla was content in knowing that at least half of the original cargo was secure.

Planning the Piracy

William Blackstock, one culprit, confirmed Bonilla's account of the events when he was interrogated by Honorable Gilbert Fleming, *Lieutenant-General-and-Commander-in-Chief* of the Leeward Islands, on 26th of November 1750.

He was on board the sailing sloop, *Christian,* while they were at sea when he told him he arrived at Ocracoke Inlet in North Carolina on or about the first of October. He found there, lying at anchor, a Spanish Galleon in distress without masts or rudder. He said he saw her unloading goods and putting them on board two sloops, the *Seaflower* and the *Mary.*

When one of the sloops was loaded and the other nearly full, an officer arrived to seize the ship for breaking bulk, because the sloops were being loaded without the Governor's permission.

Before Colonel Innes and the Spanish captain were gone to Newburgh, about forty leagues away, Owen Lloyd proposed to Blackstock that he joined him and some others to carry away the two loaded sloops. He said he would go in one and his brother, John Lloyd, would go in the other, but he didn't believe him and thought it was a joke.

After the Spanish Captain left with the officer, Blackstock said, '*He yielded to the solicitations'* of Owen Lloyd and agreed to take possession of one of the vessels. It was captained by Zebulon Wade, a man from Boston who Bonilla hired.

Blackstock said that Wade, persuaded by Owen Lloyd, consented, but was asked to remain in his cabin and pretend he was unaware of what was going to happen. Owen Lloyd then took the command of the vessel upon himself, and all agreed to the plan, including John Lloyd, Owen's brother, who had a wooden leg. He was to carry away the other sloop.

The 'Pirates'

On the 9th day of October, when the transfer was completed, both boats cut their cables and headed for the open sea, leaving the bewildered Spaniards behind.

William Blackstock told Governor Fleming that he was advised to assume the name of William Davidson, but that was not his real name.

Blackstock was born in the town of Dumfries in Scotland and was Master of a sloop that sailed from Rhode Island about the latter end of September 1750.

While these men committed an act of piracy, they were not typical pirates that made a career in capturing ships and causing mayhem. Their crime was one of opportunity.

John Amrhein Jr., the author of *Treasure Island: The Untold Story*, located all the names of the men onboard the *Seaflower* after searching the archives of almost every nation.

1. Owen Lloyd was Master of the sloop
2. Trevet, born in North Carolina, acted as Mate
3. Zebulon Wade, 33 years, was Captain and part owner
4. James Moorehouse was from Connecticut
5. William Dames
6. Abraham Pritchett, was 19 years old
7. James Matthews, his alias was McMahan
8. Thomas Hobson, was the cabin boy, aged 14 years
9. William Blackstock, a Scotsman with one eye
10. Charles McClair, his alias, was Old Livingston
11. Enoch Collins and;
12. Jonathan Deacon

Finding a Proper Place to Share the Booty

Since they were out at sea and no one on board was acquainted with the West Indies, except for Owen Lloyd, he undertook to carry them to places there where they might safely share and dispose of the effects on board. On that account, and as the chief contriver of the design, they gave the command of the vessel to Lloyd.

He then proposed to go to the French Island of Saint Barthelemy, but the first land he made was Spanish Town, which they took for. Afterwards, they fell to Leeward of that amongst the Anegada shoals. When they stood off to sea to clear the reefs, they fell in with the Danish Island of St. Croix.

There, they disposed of some of the money, but not knowing what to do with so large a treasure, they looked to Lloyd who knew the area. He advised them to go to Norman Island, one of the little islands near Tortola, about forty miles away. Lloyd thought it would be a perfect place to share their booty on shore; some of which may still be concealed.

Unloading the Sloop

When they anchored there and unloaded the sloop, they found in her:

- Fifty chests of dollars, containing each three bags, and each bag a thousand dollars.

- Two boxes of about three feet long, two feet broad and a foot and a half deep, containing church plate and other wrought silver.

- One hundred and twenty bales of cochineal containing approximately two hundred pounds in each bag and,

- Seventeen bags of indigo, a quantity of hides, chests of vanilla, and sixty bags of tobacco stems.

Splitting The Spoils

All the cargo was distributed in the manner following viz:

- Five chests of dollars to Owen Lloyd as Master and pilot of the sloop from Carolina.

- Five to Capt. Wade who was the Commander of the sloop until they left Carolina and,

- Four to each of the other persons aboard, with the rest equally divided amongst them.

All carried their chests on shore to bury them, except the one called by the Christian name of James. He kept all his onboard.

Captain Lloyd and Captain Wade reserved each one chest on board, while most of them left their cochineal in the sloop.

Blackstock and Dames took their whole dividend out, except Blackstock's share of the plate, which he left on board.

This information is important to consider, especially when calculating what was eventually found on shore and what may still lay hidden.

Thomas Wallis ~ A Witness

On November 3, 1750, a man by the name of Thomas Wallis spotted Lloyd's sloop and approached his vessel in his open-decked coble.

Wallis was likely a fisherman checking on his fish traps nearby.

According to Blackstock's confession, Wallis went on board and demanded of Lloyd, *'What is your business here? Why did you not anchor in the Road?'*

Marooning the Men

Alarmed by the invasive questions, Lloyd responded by pretending that they had '*come to stop a leak,*' hoping Wallis would go away quietly.

As soon as he did, he weighed anchor and sailed away, leaving Dames and Charles on shore to fend for themselves. Lloyd left them with no provisions or other necessaries of life, effectively marooning them.

It was discovered later that Lloyd had absconded to the Danish Island of St. Thomas and left the *Seaflower* anchored there before he proceeded to the island of St. Croix. There, he purchased a new sloop before heading to the island of Sint Eustatius.

Blackstock, having no other choice, went with Thomas Wallis in his coble to Tortola to find the President to tell him about what had transpired.

He reluctantly informed him of the goods his shipmates hid.

- Twenty bags of cochineal,
- Two bags of indigo, and
- A quantity of tobacco, which he tried to convince him was worthless. All of which, he told him; they had gotten out of a wreck off the coast of North Carolina.

President Abraham Chalwill, who had the command of the island since President Purcell was away, said he would go over and see if the tobacco was worth anything.

Chalwill, a man of fifty-nine years, was described as *"a gentleman with an unblemished character of loyal principles, a steady friend, and a worthy member of the community."* He sailed over to Norman Island and found the tobacco to be as Blackstock had represented it.

Shallop sketched by Gordon Grant

"Then, going from the place where the tobacco was to another part of the bay, Chalwill found Blackstock's cochineal. However, several people who had *discovered or heard of the dollars were busy looking for and seizing them."*

Blackstock reported that *'he did not know how the people came to discover or come to the knowledge thereof.'*

When the President found the cochineal, he turned to Charles and reportedly said, *"Old man, if you have any money, bring it out and I will take care of it for you, or these people will take your life for it."*

Regrettably, Charles brought six bags of dollars and gave them to the President, which he guarded himself the entire night, until the next day, when the President brought it over to Tortola.

When a vessel entered the bay, the President hired him immediately to transport the cochineal.

Charles then brought out three more bags of money, which were put on board together with the cochineal.

Proclamations to Apprehend the Pirates

Afterwards, the President, who believed the information Blackstock gave him, that he had gotten the dollars and cochineal out of a wreck, returned everything back to him.

Blackstock and Dames then bought a shallop for a thousand dollars and left Tortola for good.

They proceeded to Sint Eustatius and went on shore to learn what they could about Captain Lloyd.

Unbeknownst to them, Governor Fleming had issued proclamations to all the islands to be on the lookout for the pirates before he escorted two companies of troops to Tortola to retrieve all he could for the rightful owners.

When Blackstock heard that Lloyd was apprehended and in custody, he sailed to Anguilla, where unfortunately for him, he too was caught and arrested.

Governor Fleming stopped there while en route to Tortola.

Under oath, Blackstock confessed and recounted the events as they unfolded.

Without his confession, no one would have known about his participation in the robbery or how his criminal activities impacted the history of the British Virgin Islands.

Robbing the Robbers

On November 4th, the people of Tortola learned of the affair, and *'crowded over to rob the robbers.'*

"Everybody concluded they had a right to as much of their good fortune that had been thrown into their possession, and the dollars went from hand to hand, and they sold the cochineal as if it was lawfully gained."

"It was difficult to bring people to reason against their interests," wrote Governor Fleming.

"The greater mischief," he emphasized, "was that they searched in bodies, were equal sharers, and most of them needy or transient people and negroes. The mass of the treasure was dissipated into such hands and was beyond recovery."

A Finder's Fee

The Ipswich Journal confirmed that, "One half the total amount of $150,000.00 found, fell to the share of the negroes who were the first discoverers of the hidden treasure." *The Ipswich Journal on June 8, 1751.*

By reminding the inhabitants of the danger of concealment, Governor Fleming convinced some of them he would prosecute all concealers and would send troops to all the islands to find them if they didn't return the stolen goods.

Using this approach, he eventually recovered a portion of the dollars. A finder's fee, whereby the people would keep a third in their hands as salvage, was sufficient, and insisted upon by the President.

Questioning the Conduct of the President

However, Governor Fleming thought it best for His Majesty's Service to suspend the President. His conduct on this occasion proved him unfit to be in command. Instead of doing his utmost to secure the treasure, he took a considerable share of the spoils.

A View of Road Town, Tortola, British Virgin Islands © The Steen Collection

Under oath, President Chalwill admitted to having in his possession over 1,400 pieces-of-eight, and Thomas Stephens, Esq., 2,460 pieces-of-eight. Both men were suspended.

In their stead, Robert Phipps, a relative of Colonel Francis Phipps who owned Norman Island, and George Nibbs Esq., the Collector for Tortola, were appointed to be on his Majesty's Council.

This decision would leave the island in the care of Bazabeel Hodge, a man of strong moral principles, and a more capable man of great fortune, resolution, and temper.

In the end, a sum of $20,429, together with a quantity of cochineal, indigo, and hides, was recovered.

The finders that turned in their silver were allowed to keep $7,514 of the money.

The Results of the Ruling

According to the opinion given in the *Naval Law Report* of June 4, 1751, the ruling left Bonilla virtually empty-handed.

They decided that *"Bonilla's effects ought to have been seized by the President and Council of Tortola immediately and restored with no other salvage fees other than for necessary charges and expenses."*

"All those persons who had received the goods were liable to restore them to their rightful owner." However, given the turn of events, it was too late to recover any more of the treasure.

This judgement was a disappointing outcome for Bonilla, who ultimately received a paltry sum for such a significant loss.

A List of the People who Turned Their Pieces-of-Eight in for a Salvage Percentage

Blackstock further confessed to authorities that two days after he went to Tortola, he secretly returned to Norman Island with Thomas Wallis to search for the silver plate but found that it was all gone.

Governor Ralph Payne's letter to the King, dated November 30, 1750, included a sample list of people that had received some of the treasure. He reported that:

- President Chalwill, Sr., had 1,400 pieces-of-eight and 5 plates
- Abraham Chalwill, Jr., the President's son, had 20 bags, or 20,000, but claimed 3,268 pieces-of-eight
- Robert Hackett had 30,000 pieces-of-eight or 30 bags
- Rebecca Purcell had 20,000, however, she later claimed 1,212 pieces-of-eight
- Mrs. Adrianna Jeff had a considerable quantity of dollars and plate (two canoe loads), but claimed 508 pieces-of-eight
- John Haynes, the Marshall, had 30 or 40 bags
- Christopher Hodge and James Pasea, 2,005
- Absolom Zigers, 605   " "
- Thomas Stephens, 2,460
- George Wickham, 3,740 " "
- William Blackstock, 1,121 " "
- John Downing, 210 " "
- William Ronan, 52 """"
- Peter Hodge, 400 " "
- Lewis Higgs, 1,640 " "
- William Pickering, 246 " "
- George Walker kept an unknown quantity, as did,
- William Dames

A view of Her Majesty's Prison in Road Town © Thomas Dixon Green

'A Fragrant Piece of Wickedness!'

It shocked the Lieutenant General when he reflected on the situation and lawlessness that had taken place on Tortola, from the common people to the Council members.

He insisted that a church, a courthouse, and a jailhouse be built on the island, all of which was absolutely necessary, according to him, for decency, order, and the internal governance of the island.

A worthy clergyman of the Church of England would be of the utmost importance as well.

As to this piracy committed, he confirmed the findings in the *Naval Law Report,* that *"as much of the treasure should have been restored as possible, and all the pirates should have been apprehended and suffer the pains which the laws of all nations inflict."*

The Governor General, Sir Ralph Payne, was angry, and called the whole affair, *'A fragrant piece of wickedness!'*

Road Harbour © The National Archives

Catching the Culprits

Catching the culprits was easier than expected. Bonilla had sent notices throughout the West Indies to be on the lookout for the pirates.

When Lloyd and some of his confederates went to St. Eustatius, it wasn't long before they were spotted and apprehended. They were seized as soon as they landed and *put into the cistern,* presumably the jail.

Deputy-Governor Gumbs of Anguilla detained them and secured a full confession of the piracy.

Their declarations were written in old Dutch, but when they were translated, they revealed a wealth of information! Recorded were their real names, their ages, where they were from, their roles aboard the sloop, and what each seaman received as his share of the unlawful prize. By Dec 14, 1750, the news traveled as far as Rhode Island that the pirates were finally in custody.

Where Did Owen Lloyd Bury Bonilla's Treasure?

For close to three hundred years, treasure hunters have been searching for the exact location where Owen Lloyd once anchored to hide away his ill-gotten gains, yet no one has publicly acknowledged finding even one coin.

If it was so easy for the inhabitants of Tortola to locate and dig up the bags of dollars and silver plate, then why has it been so difficult for searchers today when they have the advantage of technology?

Could all the treasure have been found and not one pillar dollar be left in the sand?

Or perhaps, it's because no one knows with certainty which bay Lloyd chose for his hiding spot, because the archival records of every nation have omitted this precious clue?

Here's what we know.

Anchored in a Suspicious Location

Thomas Wallis, a fisherman, spotted Lloyd's vessel when the crew were unloading the cargo on or about November 3, 1750.

Had it not been for the inquisitive actions of Wallis, there would be no lucky finders on that hazy November day.

When Wallis approached the vessel and asked Lloyd, *"Why did you not anchor in the road?"* Wallis was obviously very suspicious about their chosen location.

Lloyd could not have been anchored in the Bight because the bay was a sheltered area where vessels commonly rode at anchor. It's given name, *Man-of-War Bay,* represented all the powerful warships and frigates that once sought refuge there.

Anchoring inside would not have aroused Wallis' suspicions. This is one reason it's believed that the Bight was not the location of Owen Lloyd's loot.

Lloyd's Possible Location

On a return visit from Money Bay many years ago, I made an interesting observation that may reveal the actual location of Lloyd's anchorage and where Wallis was when he spotted the *Seaflower*.

One day, as I rounded the western end of Norman Island to head to Money Bay for a day of exploring, I noticed a couple of fishermen checking on their fish traps. At first, I thought nothing of it, but on subsequent occasions when I was en route to Money Bay again, I saw a local fishing boat again at this same location.

I wondered, Could this be where Thomas Wallis was fishing when he spotted Lloyd's boat in Money Bay?

If this location was a popular fishing spot today, could it have been just as fruitful in the year 1750?

I surmise Wallis was likely setting or hauling his fish traps at this particular location when he noticed the *Seaflower* anchored in the cove. From his vantage point, marked with an X on the map, he could have seen clearly into Money Bay, approximately two miles away.

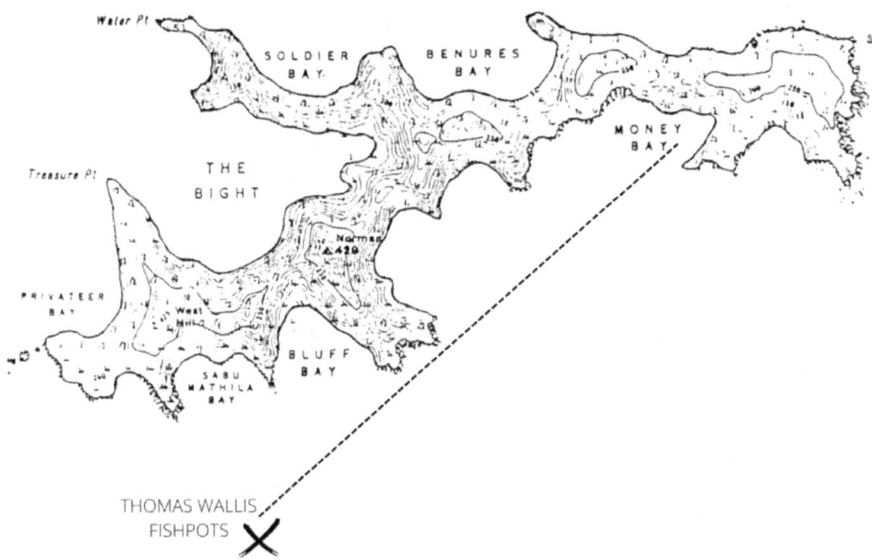

Spotting them would have made him 'sufficiently suspicious' to have the 'confidence' to approach an unknown vessel and 'demand' of its occupants what they were doing there.

This premise supports the theory that Money Bay was likely the location for Lloyd's loot. Below are a few more arguments to support Money Bay as the burial location of Bonilla's Treasure.

The Meaning Behind the Moniker, Money Bay

Second, if you'll notice, many of the islands in the British Virgin Islands are named intentionally for their appearance, their produce, a person of distinction, or with the US Islands of St. Thomas and St. John, a Christian saint.

The island of Jost van Dyke, for instance, was named for a Dutch privateer by the same name. Peter Island, according to Dr. Michael D. Kent, the author of *Twice She Struck, The Story of RMS Rhone*, was named for the '*beautified disciple.*'

Following are the origins of the names of a few of the islands:

- Salt Island was named for its indigenous mineral
- Fallen Jerusalem, had the appearance of broken rocks reminiscent of the Fallen City or Old Jerusalem
- Dead Chest for its likeness to a coffin
- The Indians, a supposed likeness to 'a group of red brown,' Indians afloat in a canoe,' (Kingsley, 1871)
- Virgin Gorda, the fat Virgin, (Columbus, 1493)
- Man-of-War Bay, for powerful war ships at anchor
- Beef Island, for its quantity of livestock
- Sandy Cay was recorded as Sandy Island in the early 1700s
- Scrub Island and Prickly Pear Island for their thorny brush
- Tortola, the Land of the Turtle Doves, (Columbus, 1493), and
- Cooper Island, reportedly named for the coopers who came to collect the white cedar used for making rum barrels.

The list goes on.

However, there was only one documented event of piracy involving the unearthing and retrieval of hard currency in the ground at Norman Island that would give rise to calling the southernmost harbour, *Money Bay*.

Money Bay on the Map

Third, another clue in support of Money Bay can be found on recently published maps of the British Virgin Islands.

Early maps of Norman Island, for example, the 1789 map drawn by Lieutenant Edward H. Columbine, who gave the bight its name, Man-Of-War Bay, and a 1793 map, have not included a survey of the eastern side of the Island, only the western end.

The likely reason being that there was not a harbour they deemed significant to include on a chart.

The southern side of the island was rough and open to the strong winds and currents. However, maps published in the early twentieth century have included the outline of the entire island and added *"Money Bay"* or *"Landing Bay"* to its southern shore.

The local populace coined Money Bay in reference to the treasure found there. It's doubtful that visiting surveyors would have known of this.

I believe the little narrow beach on the southeastern side of the island to be Lloyd's location, unless modern day maps are incorrect.

In fact, the earliest recorded reference to "Money Bay" was in 1897 by H.O. Creque. He confirmed, *"One of the bays on the coast has been aptly nicknamed 'Money Bay.'"*

A Confession About the Cochineal

Blackstock's confession about where his cochineal could be found seems to thwart some researchers into believing that their anchorage had to be a large bay, like the Bight, but I don't believe this is so.

The bags of cochineal weighed about two hundred pounds each. With one hundred and twenty bags on board, they would have been removed from the vessel after the tobacco, which one would suspect was stored on top of the crates. Blackstock is quoted as saying:

> *"Then, going from the place where the tobacco was, to another part of the bay, he there found this Examinant's cochineal."*

The area behind Money Bay is large enough to support the conclusion that the portion of cochineal belonging to Blackstock could have been dragged further inland to another location, possibly behind the swamp, instead of nearer the beach.

Out of Sight of Prying Eyes

Have you ever played the popular game, *Hide and Seek*, where one player closes his or her eyes for a moment, while the other players hide, then the seeker opens his eyes and tries to find the hiders?

Think about where you hid as a child if you played this game.

Did you hide in an obvious place where you might be spotted or was it *behind* an object, like the sofa, or wrapped *inside* the curtains, or perhaps, *under* a table?

Human nature has changed little over the years. For this reason, it is highly likely that Owen Lloyd and his band of pirates concealed their treasures on the southern side of the island… *out of sight of prying eyes.*

Captain Kidd's Hidden Treasure

Let's look at where a famous privateer buried his treasure.

Captain Kidd hid one of his caches on Gardiner's Island in 1697, one of few documented caches buried on a private island.

When he did so, he reportedly placed his cache down in a hollow, close to a ravine, one mile behind the beach. From a tree he used as a marker, it was so many feet, so many degrees, down in the Cherry Hill Field.

Kidd attempted to hide it out of sight of anyone in the harbor, but he allegedly allowed John Gardiner, the owner of the island, to be an eyewitness to its location.

Kidd buried upwards of $30,000 worth of jewels, including hundreds of diamonds, gems, rubies, sapphires, together with silver and gold bars!

There it lay for two years because Kidd threatened the life of Gardiner's family. He reportedly said to Gardiner, *"If I come back for this treasure and it is not here, I will have your head, or your son's."*

Hiding the sloop *behind* Norman Island in a secret hidden cove was helpful for Lloyd. It would have allowed the crew the time each man needed to tuck away four chests, without worrying about being seen.

A Clue to the Treasure's Location

Further evidence to support Money Bay being the location of Lloyd's loot can be found in William Blackstock's confession.

There was one clause where I believe Blackstock revealed more than he realized. He said…

> *"While he was on the island, several people who had discovered or heard of the dollars were busy looking for and seizing them."*

> *"He did not know how they came to discover or come to the knowledge thereof."*

Blackstock knew their vessel could not have been seen by anyone from Tortola or from the Sir Francis Drake Channel.

When they departed St. Croix and arrived at Norman Island, they were headed north.

This placed them *behind* Norman Island on the southern side of the island, completely out of view of everyone.

That's why he was surprised about how the people of Tortola could have known.

Road Town, Tortola © The Sheen Collection

Blackstock must have realized that the island residents were probably told the location of their anchorage by Thomas Wallis and/or by President Chalwill.

After all, both Wallis and Chalwill were at their location the day before the inhabitants discovered the news.

Blackstock would not have made the comment in the first place, that he *'did not know how they came to discover or come to the knowledge thereof'* if they had anchored in Privateer's Bay, the Bight, Soldier's Bay, or Benure's Bay, because those bays are all open and exposed to the Sir Francis Drake Channel.

He would have realized immediately that they must have been spotted.

When the President found the cochineal on the island and said to Charles, *"Old man, if you have any money, bring it out and I will take care of it for you or these people will take your life for it,"* he could see the sailing craft heading towards their location, probably rounding the western end of Norman Island.

Charles then retrieved six more bags of dollars and gave them to the President. When Captain Purser entered the bay, he too must have heard of the discovery and went to see the location for himself. It was only by chance that the President used him to transport the cochineal to Tortola.

The Perfect Beach for Privacy

Ironically, even today, if a vessel is spotted anchored in Money Bay, it will raise suspicions and make one question the captain's intentions.

In June 1999, a smuggler from the island of St. Maarten dropped a group of 24 illegal immigrants off at Money Bay. The people allegedly paid the captain to bring them to the US Virgin Islands, but finding it too risky, he dropped them off there, where *no one would spot them.* They reportedly found Spanish bibles on the ground after they were rescued. Money Bay was and still is the perfect secluded little beach for privacy.

The Value of the Silver

In November 1750, the pirates buried 44 wooden chests of Spanish dollars on Norman Island, an equivalent of 132,000 pieces-of-eight.

Factors such as rarity, condition, demand, economic conditions, and the story behind the coin affects its value, so it's impossible to say exactly how much one of these coins would be worth today.

When word spread about the discovery of some of those silver dollars, imagine all the canoe-rigged crafts beating back and forth through the strong currents to be the first to get to the island.

If it were not for Wallis tending to his fish traps on that hot and humid November afternoon, no one would have been the wiser or the richer on that fateful day.

Main Street, Road Town, Tortola © Thomas Dixon Green

Reburied in their Backyards

The clues speak for themselves: The location of a popular fishing spot with a straight view into Money Bay; the nickname given to the area; the maps identifying the beach; the characteristics of human nature, previous clandestine activity, and finally, Blackstock's sincere surprise on how anyone could have discovered their location.

Taken all together, the evidence is overwhelming and lends great credibility to Money Bay on the southeastern side of Norman Island as the burial location of Bonilla's lost treasure.

Money Bay holds the key to the greatest treasure hunt ever undertaken by the people of Tortola, who it was said '*made a fine haul of it.*'

Interestingly, more bags of Bonilla's treasure may be found in Road Town, reburied in the backyards of those who robbed the robbers. Perhaps Robert Louis Stevenson was right. '*There is still more treasure, not yet lifted.*'

Chapter 4

The Sinking of HMS Santa Monica 1782

Thirty-two years after the discovery of one of the largest buried treasures in the Caribbean, Norman Island was once again, the focus of the town gossip.

His Majesty's frigate, *HMS Santa Monica* was sailing along the island's southern shore when she suddenly hit an uncharted rock.

The submerged pinnacle was located two miles southwest of Norman Island's western coast and rose from the depths to within nine feet of the surface.

On April 18, 1782, Captain Willkie of the *Mary* delivered the despatch to Bristol with the 'disagreeable intelligence'.

Capt. John Linzee, Royal Navy, 1775

The Santa Monica was lost, but the people have been saved.

John Linzee, an experienced naval officer, was the captain of the *Santa Monica*.

His leadership was credited with saving much of the stores, and cargo, and all but one of the crew members.

HMS Santa Monica

According to a research report by *East Carolina University,* the vessel was on patrol from Antigua with orders to retaliate against five American ships that had recently attempted to raid Tortola.

While in convoy, *Santa Monica* "struck heavy four times and in the space of two minutes, she bulged on an unknown rock."

The 202-man crew employed five pumps and forty buckets to stop the rushing water from filling the hull.

Snorkeling Over a Shipwreck

To save the ship, Captain Linzee had to make a quick decision, so he ran the 145-foot vessel towards the shore on the island of St. John.

Despite their best efforts, the ship broke up rapidly, removing any hope of making repairs.

There she sat on the bottom for over 188 years, until the summer of 1970, when an employee of the *Caribbean Research Institute* at the College of the Virgin Islands discovered the ships' remains while snorkeling.

John Roy, to whom the credit was given, spotted the remnants lying in 25 feet of water, approximately 100 yards offshore in Round Bay. Excavation of the site began the following year to learn about the archaeological history of the artifacts.

It's no surprise they found evidence of looting, but the team was able to safeguard some of the pottery, glass bottles, and various metal fittings from the ship for preservation. Their discovery fit the profile they surmised of a vessel being beached in an emergency.

What remains today is a treasure trove…. *a time capsule* cemented in crustaceans on the bottom that have frozen the historical fragments together forever.

Perhaps in the future, technology will reveal the full story behind the terrifying experience the crew endured as they struggled to keep their ship afloat on that fateful day.

The story of the HMS *Santa Monica* adds a rich chapter to the island's maritime history and deserves a prominent place in the history books.

Chapter 5

Prospecting for Treasure on Peter Island ~ 1865

R umours of a buried treasure on Peter Island have been circulating for over 200 years.

Ever since a distinguished visitor published his remarks about meeting an old inhabitant of the island that was said to be worth £60,000 pounds sterling, residents have been searching for its location.

Captain Thomas Southey, a prolific writer and historian, was a Commander of the Royal Navy.

He served in the West Indies as part of the British campaign to achieve naval dominance in the Caribbean during the Napoleonic Wars. (1803-1815)

As a matter of interest, he authored *The Chronological History of the West Indies,* which was published in 1827.

In 1806, his vivid description of his encounter with a local planter and his family captured the attention of readers, wondering where this farmer could have found his wealth, and better yet, where did he bury it before his death?

The planter told the captain he lived first on Tortola for twenty years, and then another twenty years on Peter Island.

William Smith was likely his name.

He was the only person to have purchased lands on Peter Island twenty years prior to the captain's arrival.

Smith became the owner of sixty acres on June 15, 1784, and added additional lands on April 21, 1785, further supporting the captain's account.

A view of Dead Chest Island and Peter Island © Thomas Dixon Green

Remarks by a Commander of the Royal Navy

Captain Southey's impressions of Peter Island were accurate.

He said, *"The island was a kind of Robinson Crusoe spot, a place where a man ought to be a farmer, doctor, carpenter, fisherman, planter, everything himself."*

"The farmer's house was only the ground floor and his roof, which was made of shingles, projected some six or eight feet beyond the sides, like that of a Quaker's hat." He remembered that:

- "Not a pane of glass was in the house, merely shutters for the apertures.

- In the center of the drawing room or hall were tied up ears of Indian corn.

- On a chair lay a fishing net, and in one corner, hung another.

- His possessions included a spyglass, a fowling piece, chairs, a looking glass, and pictures of the four seasons."

- "The library, he remarked, comprised a prayer book, an almanack, and one volume of the Naval Chronicle.

- On the left-hand side, was a room with a range of machines for extracting the seeds from cotton, and around the house could be found an abundance of goats, turkeys, fowls, bulls, cows, pigs, dogs, and cats."

Southey must have thought, what an odd assortment of accouterments for a life on a desolate isle?

The old gentleman made quite an impression on him. The planter, he said, was dressed in a large, wide-brimmed white hat, which appeared to have been in use for half a century.

His house was in a place that would make a man feel its comforts whenever the weather was bad. It was placed on an inferior eminence, commanding a view of the bay, only a musket shot from the precipice.

A Turtle Dove

The family supported themselves by cultivating ground provisions which they supplemented with turtle doves, a small edible bird from the pigeon family.

The old man boasted that in one shooting season of three months, he caught five hundred and forty pigeons himself.

After his wife died, it reportedly moved to Norman Island. If that was true, then William Smith may likely have been a relation of John Rogers Smith, who leased a portion of Norman Island together with Abraham Chalwill Hill.

There, Smith lived in the pirate's den for the rest of his days as a hermit, unable to spend his fortune. Some believe his treasure may still lie hidden on either Peter Island or Norman Island, awaiting the lucky fortune finder.

A Tale of Buried Treasure

There's no doubt that Peter Island has a unique history of its own.

The island was first granted to James George, Esq. on February 21, 1714, by Daniel Smith, the Lieutenant-Governor of Nevis. A bay on the southwestern side of the island was named for him, called *James George's Bay.*

Peter Island also has its own tales of buried treasure, perhaps not as widely known as those about Norman Island.

You can find them, if you're lucky, scattered throughout the archival records of various institutions. Many are forgotten stories of half-hearted treasure hunts to faraway places, thrown together to entertain the reading public.

There was an interesting article titled, *Fortunate End of a Wild Goose Chase,* that was published in the *Pittsburg Post* in 1895. It was about a treasure hunting expedition that allegedly took place on Peter Island around 1865.

This account contained remarkable similarities and landmarks that lend credibility to the tale.

Charles B. Lewis

The author, Charles B. Lewis (1842-1924), was a prolific writer and humorist, publishing entertaining editorials weekly throughout his career.

Lewis wrote the following story from the point of view of the captain's young nephew as he, and his aunt and uncle, embarked on an exciting adventure in search of buried riches.

It began...

Fortunate End of a Wild Goose Chase ~ 1895

"My uncle, Captain Abel Jones, was fifty years of age and had retired from the sea when he met a man who asked for a place to stay.

It did not take half an eye to see that he was a sailor and during the conversation; he learned of his surprising adventures in the West Indies.

He gave his name as John Drake. When they had talked of ships and sailors and gales and calm for a couple of hours, the stranger suddenly turned to my uncle and confided,

> *"See here mate, you have made me welcome and used me like a man, and I'm a good mind to put you in the way of a good thing."*

> *"Send the boy to bed and get rid of the old woman, and I'll tell you something to open your eyes."*

'The boy' strongly objected to going off to bed at that juncture, and as for the "old woman," who was, of course, my Aunt Hetty, she plumped herself down between the two men with her knitting work and grimly observed:

"What you have to say to Abe can be said before his family or not at all!"

"I don't think Drake had any other object than to find lodgings, but discovering that Uncle Abel was rather credulous, he conceived a plan.

He was only about forty years of age, but there seemed to be something wrong with him as a sailor."

"After many mysterious nods, winks, and chuckles to arouse our curiosity, and after obliging the three of us to hold up our right hands and swear never to reveal the secret to a mortal man, he reeled off his yarn.

Aside from many other voyages, he had made several trips from New York and Boston to the West Indies. On one of these trips, which was his last voyage, he had befriended a sick and dying sailor in Puerto Rico.

When the man found that he must die, he told Drake of a treasure of $300,000 in gold buried out on one of the Virgin Islands, lying to the eastward on the island of St. Thomas."

The Treasure's Location

"There was the usual rough map drawn by a sailor's hand, but Drake had lost this.

He remembered, however, that the treasure was on Peter Island, and that one must step off 21 paces from a certain tree toward a certain great rock.

The dying sailor had not been a pirate, but a mutineer, and the treasure had come from an English vessel which was carrying the gold to one of the Bahamas to pay a government claim.

I can't remember all the details as Drake related them, but he was a smooth-tongued and plausible liar and made out a fine story. He was sure the gold was still there, and he had been waiting to find someone who would deal honestly with him.

My Uncle, Abel, drank in and believed every word the liar uttered, but not so with Aunt Hetty. She sized the man up for what he was and plainly told him he was yarning."

Danish Museum © Det Kgl. Bibliotek ~ 1865

"He pretended to be much grieved at her suspicions, and when he went off to bed, he said he would go to Kennebunk, Maine and try to find some ship owner or captain who would bring the treasure off and make a fair divide.

There was $300,000 in coined gold, and all he wanted for himself was $25,000.00.

The following morning, after Drake had retold his yarn and added to it, Aunt Hetty weakened in her objections, and finally came to believe there was something in it."

A Strange Voyage

"Before the day was over, she was as enthusiastic as Uncle Abel, and that was the beginning of what I have termed *a strange voyage*.

During a couple of days, the captain and Drake went over to Kennebunk to look for a suitable craft and found the brig *Foam* for sale."

"The captain drew his last dollar from the bank, mortgaged his farm, sold off three cows, forty sheep, ten hogs, and a yoke of oxen, and raised the money to buy her.

As everybody knew he had given up the sea, this move of his was productive of great gossip.

When it was known that Aunt Hetty was about to go along, the gossip increased. Drake got drunk and boasted of the treasure, and so it came about that everybody knew the object of our quest, though no one knew where we were going.

Capt. Jones was called a fool by his best friends, but neither ridicule nor abuse had any effect on him.

By the time he was ready for sea, he was a firm believer that he would return with money enough to buy out all Kennebunk. His wife was even more enthusiastic.

We shipped a mate and four sailors on the 'lay' plan. Each was to have a certain percent of the treasure, if found. Aunt Hetty was to act as a cook. This gave us seven men, and I went along as cabin boy.

The brig sailed for Boston, got a cargo for Puerto Rico, and we were finally off.

We were hardly clear of the land when trouble arouse. Drake wanted to live in the cabin and play passenger instead of doing duty as a sailor, and Aunt Hetty started out to boss everyone around in a way that upset them.

The mate, whose name was Furbish, had forgotten his instruments, and Capt. Jones had bought some old water casks, but most of their contents had leaked out before we left the wharf."

The Battered Brig

"We were four days out. We had to hail an incoming ship and buy two casks of water, and within a week, Aunt Hetty's economy left us without tea or coffee.

It has always been a marvel to the seafaring men of Kennebunk that the battered brig reached her port of destination.

Captain Jones was an old-fashioned sailor who made his way almost altogether by dead reckoning.

He could get the latitude of the sun at noonday after a tremendous struggle, but when he had worked out his sights, he wasn't sure of his position within fifty miles.

The brig's sails were old, the rigging sadly out of repair, and her foremasts were so insecure that only about half the usual amount of sail was spread.

It was pure luck that she ever reached Puerto Rico, even though she made the longest passage on record.

She was hardly in port before Drake deserted and shipped on a craft bound for Liverpool.

The sailors disliked him, and strong hints had been thrown out that if the treasure was not found, it would be worse for him.

The man's desertion made no difference in our plans.

Uncle Abel and Aunt Hetty were certain they could find the buried gold without his help, and when the matter was talked over, everybody was happy that he departed, because there would be $25,000 more to divide up among the rest."

Peter Island © Thomas Dixon Green

Anchoring off Peter Island

"When the cargo had been discharged, the brig started for Peter Island.

The Virgin group lay dead to the east, and yet, Captain Jones missed it and run 100 miles into the Atlantic before he figured out what had happened.

Then, he turned back and almost came very near to wrecking his craft on the reefs of Sombrero. After many days, we came to anchor off the east coast of Peter Island.

Drake had described a certain bay.

While he had never seen it, we found a bay answering close to the description.

The beach on the north side of this bay was something like the one he had told us of, but there was no tree nor rock where he had placed them."

Prospecting Ashore

"It was decided to go ashore and prospect, however, an examination of the shore resulted in a stay of three weeks, during which there was some lively digging.

We might have remained longer but for the trouble between the captain and his wife.

When the long search and hard work brought nothing, Aunty Hetty called him an idiot and bewailed their financial ruin.

Uncle Abel fired up and talked back, and they had it hot and heavy for an hour or two.

At last, the captain said he was going home. His wife declared she would stay until she found some gold.

Everybody was drawn into the quarrel and Captain Jones and three of the men took the yawl and started off, and it left four of us with the brig.

I must explain that the captain's move was made with a view of bulldozing his wife. He expected to be called back and to see Aunt Hetty knuckle down, and when nothing of the sort happened, he concluded to coast around the island and make a further search for the treasure.

A gale of wind blew them out upon the broad Atlantic, and for fourteen days they looked upon themselves as doomed.

They had but little water and provisions, lost their mast and sail the first day, and within a week, were driven to cut up their boots and chew the leather."

Drifting for Weeks

"On the fourteenth day, when all were ready to give up, they came across the bark, *North Star*. You may have read that this craft, belonging to Boston, came out of Havana with the yellow fever aboard.

She had a crew of eight men, and she was hardly clear of Abaco Island, when the captain, mate and two others died, and the survivors got out on a boat and abandoned her.

They landed on the Florida coast, while the bark, loaded with sugar, drifted out to sea. It was this craft; Capt. Jones and his men ran across after she had been drifting for three weeks.

It is a matter of record that the four men, after sailing her all over the Atlantic, and meeting with a hundred adventures, finally took a pilot 150 miles off Sandy Hook and got the bark safely into New York.

Capt. Jones got $11,000 salvage money as his share, which was $3,000 more than the *Foam* cost him.

My Aunt Hetty did not believe that Uncle Abel meant to leave us and the brig, but when the gale came on, all of us felt sure the four men had met their deaths.

We did not work for five days.

Then, feeling that the disaster had overtaken the quartet, and that she was a widow, Aunt Hetty wiped away her tears and stirred around.

She still believed in the treasure's existence. I had failed to find it because we had not looked in the right spot."

Looking for the Lone Tree

"By her orders, we weighed anchor and coasted around to the north of the island. Then we opened another bay and cast anchor.

The beach was of sand and about fifty feet wide.

Back of it was a thick growth of forest. There was a lone tree on the beach, just above the high-water mark, but no rock, as described by Drake. Aunt Hetty decided we should go to work.

One man paced off twenty-one paces in three directions, and we dug. When nothing was found, we tried fourteen paces, then seven, then dug up the tree itself.

We dug up the entire beach before we left off, or at least so thoroughly prodded it with iron rods, we felt sure nothing of value lay buried in the sands.

We were working there fifteen days before we gave up. Aunt Hetty wanted to try another place, but the two Kennebunk sailors had had enough of it and wanted to go home.

There was a settlement of fisherman on the north side of the island and almost every day, a boat had visited us.

The people knew what we were after and laughed and ridiculed us.

The idea was to get three or four fishermen to help navigate the brig to Puerto Rico where we could replace them, but as soon as they found we were short-handed; they refused to ship unless they were paid $3 a day apiece.

Aunt Hetty was a purser and a cook, and she said she'd let the brig rot at her moorings before she'd be robbed."

Prodding the Sand

"Our great good luck came out of a quarrel. Aunt Hetty got angry because we refused to do more digging and attempted to give me a whipping.

When I ran from her, she took the small boat and put off for the brig, leaving the three of us' ashore.

This happened one afternoon. The two men lay down in the shade to sleep, while I walked along the beach to gather shells.

In going to the west, and after walking about two miles, carrying one of the iron rods on my shoulder as a weapon, I came upon a smaller bay than the one the brig was lying in.

At the head of this bay was another sandy beach, and in the center of the beach, just at high water mark, stood a big rock all by itself.

I advanced to this rock and finally climbed upon it.

I had given up all thoughts of the treasure, and why the idea came to me to make a search here, I cannot tell.

I first paced seven steps to the west and probed the sand. Then I made it 14, then 21. Then returned to the rock and paced to the east.

At the third trial, or at 21 paces, I was close to a large tree which had lost most of its branches in a hurricane.

I began prodding on the north side of it, where some of the roots were exposed, and I hadn't worked five minutes before I struck something to make my heart jump."

Digging up the Treasure

"I knew it wasn't a shell or a stone by the feel of it, and it didn't occur to me that it might be a plank, or a beam washed up by the sea. So sure was I, that I had struck a treasure box, that I flung down the rod and ran away to fetch the sailors and the shovels.

What did my discovery amount to?

Well, we took from under the roots of that tree, four iron-banded boxes full of Spanish dollars, being $24,000 in all.

The money, judging from the dates on the coins and the condition of the boxes, had been buried for at least twenty years (around 1845) and whether by a pirate or someone else, we did not care. We got it aboard the brig and got the brig to Puerto Rico with no one being the wiser. Then, we sailed for home, with Aunt Hetty acting as boss of all hands.

We got safely home and out of a Tom Fool's errand and a dozen; my relatives secured a fortune in ready cash!"

An Incredible Find!

Following the clues given in this story, Aunt Hetty's sailing vessel would have been anchored in Deadman's Bay, and the treasure found by young Charles was roughly two miles away in Sprat Bay.

Imagine twenty-four thousand doubloons buried in the beach under the exposed roots of a wind-blown tree? What an incredible find if this story has some validity!

Since they dated the coins to around 1845, this treasure cache would not be old enough to be attributed to William Smith, the old planter that Captain Southey met in 1806. Smith's cache may still lay buried… *Somewhere.*

Chapter 6

Robert Louis Stevenson's Treasure Island ~ 1883

Robert Louis Stevenson, 1850 - 1894

I t all began with a map!

That's what Stevenson confided to his friend, William Henley, when he told him about his new novel.

"It's about buccaneers and buried gold, a treasure, a mutiny, and a derelict ship ... and a doctor, and a sea-cook with one leg with the chorus, *'yo-ho-ho and a bottle of rum,'*

... If this don't fetch the kids, why, they have gone rotten since my day."

Ironically, these remarks that Stevenson made over one hundred years ago mirror the true story about the loss of *La Nuestra Señora de Guadalupe* in 1750.

You'll recall that the *Guadalupe* was a 'derelict ship', laden with treasure before her crew mutinied, her cargo stolen by pirates, (one of whom had a wooden leg), and later, three of them marooned on a deserted island in the West Indies!

These similarities support the idea that Norman Island was the inspiration behind *Treasure Island,* but Stevenson said his idea for the novel came while he was painting with his stepson, Samuel Lloyd Osbourne.

Stevenson always loved maps, and during a picture-making time with Lloyd, he had drawn a fine one.

'The shape of it', he said, *'took my fancy beyond expression.'*

"Immediately, the island began to take life and swarm with people."

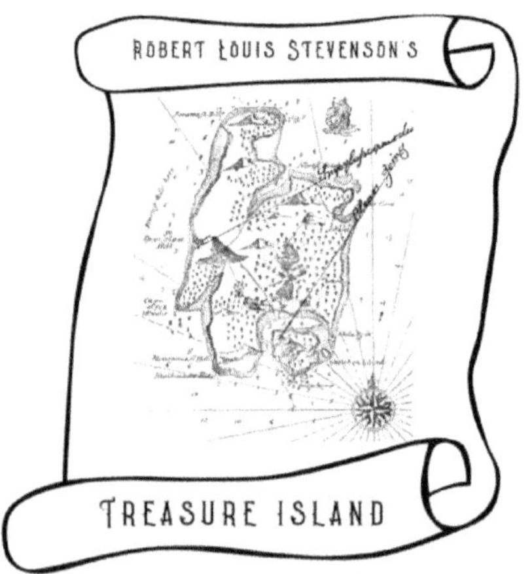

The Island Came Alive!

"All sorts of strange scenes began to take place upon the island, and as I gazed at my map, I discovered the plot," Stevenson wrote.

"I arrived at my destination, and down I sat one morning to the unfinished tale ….*and behold,* it flowed from me like small talk.

In a second tide of delighted industry, and again at the rate of a chapter a day, I finished *Treasure Island.*

It contained harbours that pleased me like sonnets, and with an unconsciousness of the predestined, I ticketed my performance, *Treasure Island.* "

I am told there are people who do not care for maps, and I find that hard to believe, he said. The name, the shapes of the woodland, the courses of the roads and rivers, the prehistoric footsteps of man still distinctly traceable up hill and down.

Somewhat in this way, as I paused upon my map of *Treasure Island,* the future chapters of the book appeared there visibly among imaginary woods.

Their brown faces and bright weapons peeped out upon me from unexpected quarters as they passed to and fro, fighting and hunting treasure on these few square inches of a flat projection.

The next thing I knew, I had some paper before me and was writing out a list of chapters.

How often have I done so, and the thing gone no farther, but there seemed elements of success about this enterprise."

A Pirate by Howard Pyle

Traditional Beliefs and Folklore

Throughout the US and British Virgin Islands and beyond, it is widely believed that Norman Island was the inspiration for Stevenson's novel.

The fairy-tale island with its deep-water coves, deserted beaches and musty caves conjures up a similar scenario to Stevenson's imaginary island. The splendor, the romance and the mystery that surrounds Norman's lofty hills and ridges are legendary.

Let's have a look at how Stevenson's *Treasure Island* came to be and the books that inspired him before exploring the similarities between the two islands.

Stevenson's Story

"It all began on a chilly September morning, by the cheek of a brisk fire, with the rain drumming on the window," Stevenson recalled. He began what he thought would be titled, *The Sea Cook*.

After reading *Tales of a Traveler*, Stevenson said, it flew up and struck him; Billy Bones, his chest, the company in the parlor, the whole inner spirit, and a good deal of the material detail of his first chapters – all were there; all were the property of Washington Irving.

"My father caught fire at once with all the romance and childishness of his original nature, he said. His own stories, that every night of his life he put himself to sleep with, dealt perpetually with ships, roadside inns, robbers, old sailors, and commercial travelers before the era of steam. Thomas Stevenson never finished one of these romances; the lucky man did not require to!

But in *Treasure Island*, he recognized something kindred to his own imagination. It was *his* kind of picturesque; and he not only heard with delight the daily chapter but set himself acting to collaborate."

Billy Bones' Sea Chest

Billy Bones was the sea-chanty-singing pirate who came plodding into the *Admiral Benbow Inn,* seeking a quiet, secluded place to stay. With an old tottering voice, he sang:

"Fifteen men on the dead man's chest -
Yo-ho-ho, and a bottle of rum!"

Stevenson described him as "a tall, strong, heavy, nut-brown man with his tarry pigtail falling over the shoulder of his soiled blue coat, his hands ragged and scarred, with black, broken nails, and a saber cut across one cheek, a dirty, livid white."

The old seaman used to be Captain Flint's first mate aboard the ship and could be rude and surly.

Billy Bones by Howard Pyle

The treasure map, tucked away in his sea chest, set the events of the novel into motion.

When the time came for Billy Bones' chest to be ransacked, Stevenson said that "his father must have passed the better part of a day preparing, on the back of a legal envelope, an inventory of its contents." Stevenson followed these exactly.

Interestingly, inside his sea chest were five or six curious 'West Indian' shells. This supports the idea of *Treasure Island's* location being in the Caribbean.

"The name of Flint's old ship – *the 'Walrus'* – was given at his father's particular request."

'No Words in My Bosom' ~ Writer's Block

For fifteen days Stevenson stuck to it, and turned out fifteen chapters: and then, in the early paragraphs of the sixteenth chapter, it ignominiously lost hold.

"My mouth was empty", Stevenson wrote, "there was not one word of *Treasure Island* in my bosom."

"I was thirty-one years of age and the head of a family. I had lost my health, and had never paid my way, never yet made £200 a year."

"My father had recently bought back and canceled a book that was judged a failure, and he thought," '*Was this to be another fiasco?'*"

"I was indeed very close to despair, but during the journey to Davos, Switzerland, where I was to spend the winter, I had the resolution to think of other things."

"But when I arrived at my destination and sat down one morning to the unfinished tale, behold," '*it flowed from me like small talk!'*"

"In a second tide of delighted industry, and again at a rate of a chapter a day, I finished *Treasure Island*.

And now, who should come dropping in, but Dr. Japp, a publisher.

My old friend, Mr. Henderson has charged him to unearth new writers for *Young Folks Magazine*."

The Missing Map

The adventures of *Treasure Island* were not quite over, though. Stevenson had written it up to the map, for the map was the chief part of his plot.

For instance, he had called an islet, *Skeleton Island,* not knowing what he meant, seeking only for the immediate picturesque. This was to justify this name: that he broke into the gallery of Mr. Poe and stole Flint's pointer.

And in the same way, it was because he had made two harbours that the *Hispaniola* was sent on her wanderings with Israel Hands.

The time came when it was decided to republish, and he sent in his manuscript, and the map along with it, to Messrs. Cassell.

The corrected proofs came back, but he heard nothing of the map. He wrote and asked and was told, '*It had never been received.*'"

"He sat aghast!"

"As you can imagine, it is one thing to draw a map at random, set a scale in one corner of it at a venture, and write up a story to the measurements. It is quite another to have to examine a whole book, make an inventory of all the allusions contained in it, and with a pair of compasses, painfully design a map to suit the data."

"He did it, and the map was drawn again in his father's office. It was embellished with blowing whales and sailing ships; and his father himself brought into service a knack he had of various writing. He elaborately forged the signature of Captain Flint, and the sailing directions of Billy Bones."

But somehow, it was never *Treasure Island* to him. As he said, the map was most of the plot. In truth, '*it was the whole plot.*'

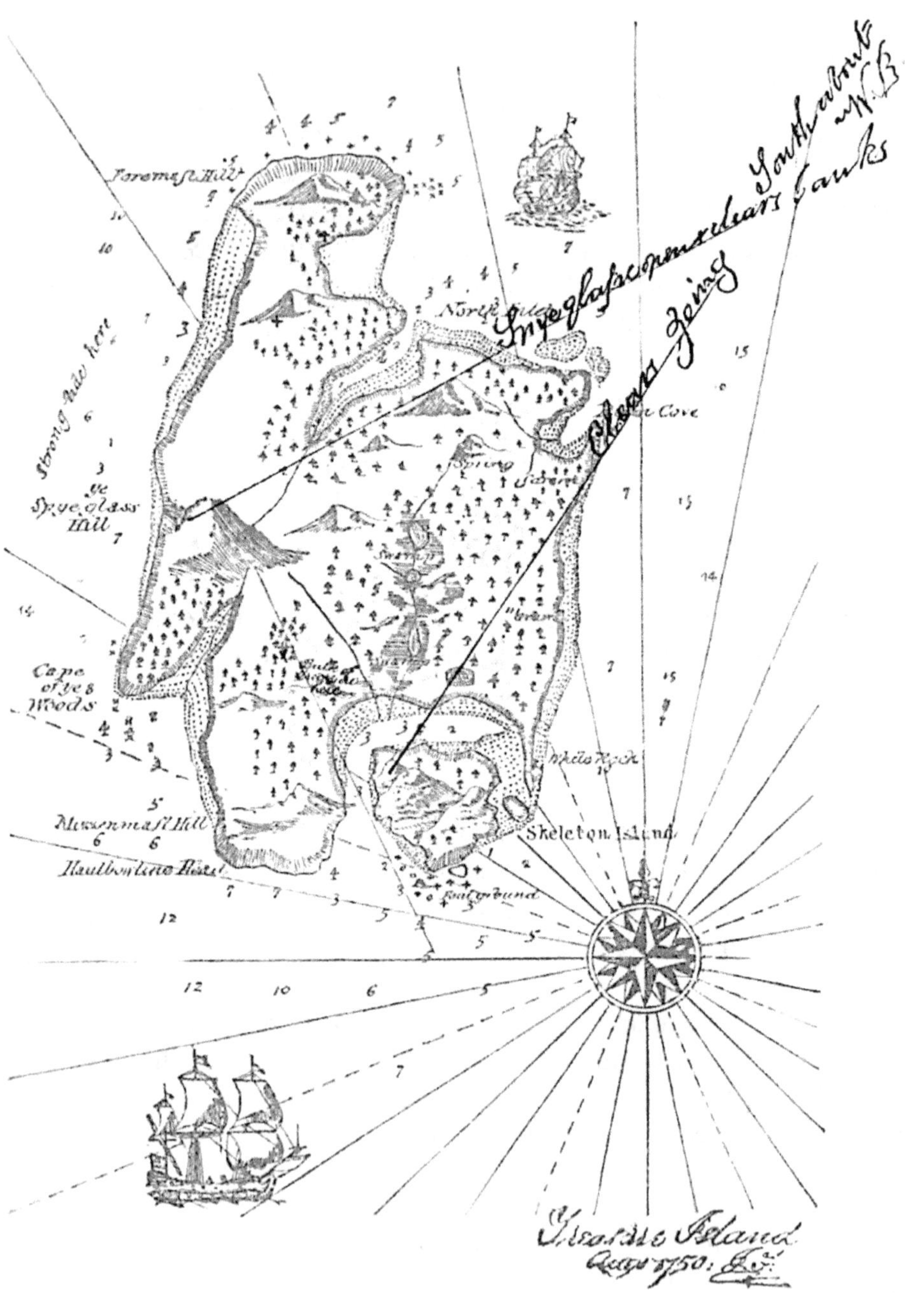

Foremast Hill
North Inlet
Snyeglasscomesheart Canks
South about
Clear going
Spye glass Hill
Spring
Cape of ye Woods
Skeleton Island
Mizzenmast Hill
Haulbowline Head
White Rock
Treasure Island
Augt 1750

Inspirations and Influences

Stevenson found value in the writings of Edgar Allan Poe, Daniel Defoe, and Washington Irving to complete *Treasure Island.*

He was also influenced by other adventure writers, like:

- Captain Charles Johnson's, *A General History of the Robberies and Murders of the Most Notorious Pirates.*

- Charles Kingsley's, *At Last: A Christmas in the West Indies,* where the name *Dead Man's Chest* originated.

- Edgar Allan Poe's, *Robinson Crusoe,* where the parrot once belonged to, and *The Gold Bug,* for the idea of the skeleton.

- Frederick Marryat's, *Masterman Ready,* for the idea of the stockade and,

- Washington Irving's, *Tales of a Traveler,* where the idea for Billy Bones and his chest originated.

In one of the forwards of his novel, he acknowledged three authors, W.G.H. Kingston, R. M. Ballantyne, and James Fenimore Cooper.

Stevenson even added some of his own recollections of canoeing on the high seas and a cruise he took on a schooner. However, the most important contribution, he said, came from the map itself, '*with its infinite, eloquent suggestion.*'

"Perhaps it is not often that a map figures so largely in a tale," he added, "yet it is always important."

"The author must know his countryside, whether real or imaginary, like his hand; the distances, the points of the compass, the place of the sun's rising and the behavior of the moon, should all be beyond cavil.

And oh, how troublesome the moon was!"

Was Norman Island the Inspiration for Stevenson's Treasure Island?

Ever since Robert Louis Stevenson published his *story for boys*, the island's location has captivated and mesmerized readers.

Locally, Norman Island is believed to be the island immortalized in *Treasure Island,* but rumours and speculation persist, keeping the suspense alive.

Robert Louis Stevenson

Curious about what the *Robert Louis Stevenson Club* knew about Norman Island, my mother and I visited Edinburgh, Scotland, in 1994 for the 100th anniversary of Stevenson's death.

There we met Dr. Alan Marchbank, President of *The Robert Louis Stevenson Club* and an expert. His warmth and kindness we've never forgotten.

Over lunch in a beautiful historic building, we shared our insights about Norman Island being Stevenson's *Treasure Island,* and if the Club was aware of what so many Virgin Islanders' believed.

To my surprise, *The Robert Louis Stevenson Club* had a different point of view. They understood that Stevenson was inspired by the moat outside his bedroom window at Heriot Row, and perhaps that is where his idea for *Treasure Island* began.

Others, however, have suggested that a favorite uncle once visited the West Indies and shared his knowledge of the islands with Stevenson when he returned.

There's no doubting Norman Island's piratical past, but was Stevenson aware of the island's history when he drew the hills and harbours of his imaginary island?

A Secret Island in the West Indies

When *Treasure Island* was first published, Stevenson was asked many times about the island's location, but he left readers curious by his response.

Stevenson reportedly said, *"I cannot tell you where it is, for I do not know."*

His tale of adventure about an expedition to a remote and secret island in the West Indies was a figment of his imagination.

When he drew the map, even he was surprised by the beauty of the harbours, which he said, *"pleased him like sonnets."*

The fictional tale itself *"flowed from him like small talk and at the rate of a chapter a day."*

Treasure Island was not a story Stevenson had to craft from beginning to end. It was a tale that came to life once the map was drawn. The characters seemed to jump from the pages as the events unfolded, and every day, Stevenson, and his family, whom he read to every evening, were delighted with the adventure.

He told his readers he could see his characters as they *"appeared there visibly among imaginary woods"* and *"peeped out at him from unexpected quarters."*

His account reminded me of my grandmother and how she authored many of her beautiful poems.

I asked her one day about her craft and the ease with which her stanzas came together so seamlessly. Her messages transcended time and spoke of love, perseverance, and faith in her Heavenly Father.

Divine Inspiration

Valerie Creque-Mawson
My maternal grandmother

She shared with me that every night she slept with a pen and paper by her bedside, because many of her poems came to her in a completed form upon awakening.

She simply jotted them down before they were forgotten.

I was perplexed. How could an entire poem be written in this way? Surely, thoughts and ideas took time to develop into the perfect verse.

When I asked my grandmother where her poetry originated, she said that her poems came from her Heavenly Father.

Could Stevenson's tale have come from the Heavenly Father as well? Is this the reason the story delighted him so? Was he 'divinely inspired' when he wrote *Treasure Island?*

There's no evidence to suggest that Stevenson ever visited the British Virgin Islands, so could he have tapped into the collective intelligence of the universe unknowingly?

We may never know the answers to these thought-provoking questions, but there's no doubt that Stevenson's treasure tale will continue to capture the hearts of many for countless generations to come.

While he said that he didn't know exactly where his *Treasure Island* was located, Stevenson gave his readers many clues, but he allegedly held back one important secret: ... *the island's bearings.*

Could Stevenson's *Treasure Island* really be written about Norman Island? Perhaps you can decide for yourself.

Here are 14 Attributes Norman Island and the British Virgin Islands have in Common with Stevenson's Treasure Island

If you've ever anchored in the Bight, hiked to Spyglass Hill, or explored the popular caves, you'll be pleasantly surprised by the uncanny resemblances between Stevenson's *Treasure Island* and Norman Island.

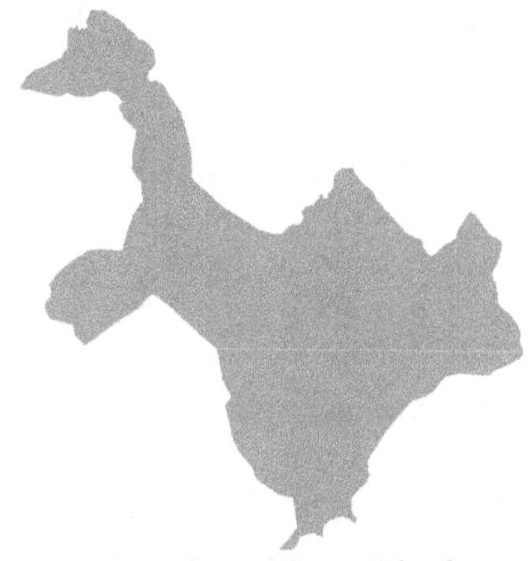

An outline of Guana Island

1. 'Like a Fat Dragon Standing Up'

- Stevenson wrote, *"It was an uninhabited island, about nine miles long and five across, shaped, you might say, like a fat dragon standing up."*

☞ References to the shape of *Treasure Island* looking like a fat dragon standing up are more in line with Guana Island off Tortola's northeast coast.

Both Guana Island and Dead Chest Island are in the same local, giving credence to Stevenson's *"Treasure Island"* being located in the British Virgin Islands.

2. Skeleton Island and the Anchorage

- "The mainland on one side and Skeleton Island on the other. The bottom was clean sand. The plunge of our anchor sent up clouds of birds wheeling and crying over the woods, but in less than a minute they were down again, and all was once more silent. "

- "We had a dreary morning's work before us, for there was no sign of any wind, and the boats had to be got out and manned, and the ship warped three or four miles round the corner of the island and up the narrow passage to the haven behind Skeleton Island. "

- "…and the anchorage, under lee of Skeleton Island, lay still and leaden as when first we entered it. The *Hispaniola*, in that unbroken mirror, was exactly portrayed from the truck to the waterline, the Jolly Roger hanging from her peak."

- "Yes, sir; Skeleton Island, they calls it. It was a main place for pirates once, and a hand we had on board knowed all their names for it. That hill to the nor'ard they calls the Fore-mast Hill; there are three hills in a row running south'ard--fore, main, and mizzen, sir."

☞ Pelican Island, with a height of 180 feet, is located at the mouth of the Bight. It fits the description perfectly of Stevenson's Skeleton Island being located *behind* the anchorage.

If you've ever been the first to drop your anchor in the Bight, you can relate to the cloud of birds that take flight after you do so. Stevenson explained the effects of the *'plunge of an anchor'* with precision, as if he had thrown the anchor himself.

The three hills referenced could be Money Bay, representing the 'Foremast', Spyglass Hill in the center, and West Hill, although slightly taller than Spyglass Hill, could be the 'Mizzen Mast'.

A view of Spyglass Hill on Norman Island © Valerie Sims

3. Spyglass Hill

- "The hills ran up clear above the vegetation in spires of naked rock. All were strangely shaped, and the Spy-Glass, which was by three or four hundred feet the tallest on the island, was likewise the strangest in configuration, running up sheer from almost every side, and then suddenly cut off at the top like a pedestal to put a statue on."

- "The outline of the Spyglass trembled through the haze, a tall pinnacle of the mountain."

- "Sheer above us rose the Spyglass, here dotted with single pines, there black with precipices."

- "But the main--that's the big un, with the cloud on it—they usually calls the Spy-glass, by reason of a lookout they kept when they was in the anchorage cleaning, for it's there they cleaned their ships, sir, asking your pardon."

According to admiralty charts, Norman Island's 'Spyglass Hill' is 429-feet high and commands a 365° sweeping view of the island's surroundings, including the harbour where ships careened.

At the top are clusters of large rocks or boulders, uniformly shaped and thick. They're like mismatched pieces of a jumbled puzzle.

Spyglass Hill is immediately recognizable on the horizon from any direction, for its center rises upwards towards the clouds, like a huge dormant volcano, similar to Stevenson's Island.

4. The Caves

- "A gentle slope ran up from the beach to the entrance of the cave. At the top, the squire met us. To me, he was cordial and kind, saying nothing of my escapade either in the way of blame or praise. At Silver's polite salute, he somewhat flushed."

- "And thereupon we all entered the cave. It was a large, airy place, with a little spring and a pool of clear water, overhung with ferns. The floor was sand. Before a big fire lay Captain Smollett, and in a far corner, only duskily flickered over by the blaze, I beheld great heaps of coin and quadrilaterals built of bars of gold."

- "For my part, as I was not much use at carrying, I was kept busy all day in the cave, packing the minted money into bread-bags."

Norman Island is home to four unique caves.

Three of them are located near Treasure Point on the western end of the island, and one is on the north shore beyond Soldier's Bay.

The latter is not a sea-cave like the others. Its entrance is located a few yards from the ocean on higher ground.

However, there is a promontory on the southern side of the Island, that could be described as a 'two-pointed hill' when viewed on a map.

Unlike Stevenson's Island, there are no caves at this location.

The mere fact, though, that large caves in which several people can enter do exist on Norman Island, add to the mounting similarities between the two locals.

5. *The Swamps*

- "Two little rivers, or rather two swamps, emptied out into this pond, as you might call it: and the foliage round that part of the shore had a kind of poisonous brightness."

☞ Just beyond the Bight, you'll find two salty, swampy ponds at the base of two hills. They fill with every heavy rainfall.

6. *The Amphitheatre*

- "The place was entirely land-locked, buried in woods, the trees coming right down to high-water mark, the shores mostly flat, and the hilltops standing round at a distance in a sort of amphitheater, one here, one there."

☞ If you're in the Bight on a quiet day, you'll understand this feeling of being in an amphitheater. The sounds echo and reverberate off the surrounding hills like you're standing in the center of a round stadium as undulating sound-waves pervade you from all sides.

7. *The Black Crag*

You can view the rock images by following the link in the QR code.

- "The bar silver is in the north cache; you can find it by the trend of the east hummock, ten fathoms south of the black crag with the face on it."

☞ Above the caves sits a large, upright rock with a 'face' carved into its surface. Its 'eyes' are slanted with the edges angled upwards. The 'mouth' is an opening to a shallow depression. I climbed up from the Bight to get a closer look, only to be held back by the thought of a deathly drop of two hundred feet to the ocean floor below. This was a dangerous climb and not recommended. Besides, you can only view the rock face from the sea below. *"The bar silver and the arms still lie, for all that I know, where Flint buried them…"*

8. *The Goats*

- "Ah," says he, "this here is a sweet spot, this island--a sweet spot for a lad to get ashore on. You'll bathe, and you'll climb trees, and you'll hunt goats, you will; and you'll get aloft on them hills like a goat yourself."

- "Ben Gunn's cave was well supplied with goats' meat, salted by himself."

- "Marooned three years agone," he continued, "and lived on goats since then, and berries, and oysters."

- "Left, left," says he; "keep to your left hand, mate Jim! Under the trees with you! Theer's where I killed my first goat."

- "What a supper I had of it that night, with all my friends around me; and what a meal it was, with Ben Gunn's salted goat and some delicacies and a bottle of old wine from the HISPANIOLA."

- "We left a good stock of powder and shot, the bulk of the salted goat, a few medicines, and some other necessaries, tools, clothing, a spare sail, a fathom or two of rope, and by the particular desire of the doctor, a handsome present of tobacco."

An island goat

☞ Norman Island has been a sanctuary for small herds of wild goats for hundreds of years.

In 1916, when their number was counted for H.O. Creque's estate, there were found to be 250 goats roaming wild on the island.

Goat meat was a necessary food source, so it's no surprise that Ben Gunn's fictional character enjoyed it too.

Turpentine Tree or Gumbo-Limbo tree © Milo44
https://commons.wikimedia.org/wiki/File:Gumbo_Limbo_Tree_DeSoto_National_Monument.JPG

9. The Red-Columned Trees

• "The first of the tall trees was reached, and by the bearings proved the wrong one. So, with the second. The third rose nearly two hundred feet into the air above a clump of underwood--a giant of a vegetable, with a red column as big as a cottage, and a wide shadow around in which a company could have maneuvered. It was conspicuous far to sea, both on the east and west and might have been entered as a sailing mark upon the chart. "

☞ The reference to the "red columned" tree is indicative of the turpentine trees or Gumbo-Limbo trees found all over Norman Island. Locally, they are known as 'tourist' trees because the bark peels off easily in patches, as if sunburned.

They can grow from 25 to 40 feet tall, and 25 to 30 feet wide, so they can appear quite large, although not as tall as those described on Stevenson's imaginary island. Fast-growing turpentine trees

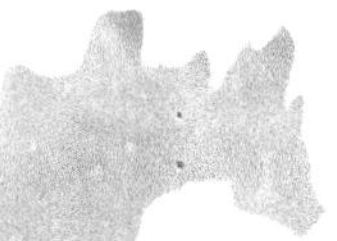

The bark

have a life span of about 100 years. With a spreading canopy of 60 feet, they can cast the perfect shadow over a hidden cache.

On June 2, 1724, Governor John Hart granted Dead Chest Island to Edward Coakley.

10. Dead Man's Chest

Fifteen men on the dead man's chest—
Yo-ho-ho, and a bottle of rum!
Drink and the devil had done for the rest—
Yo-ho-ho, and a bottle of rum!

Stevenson acknowledged Charles Kingsley, who sailed through the British Virgin Islands in the late 1860s, for the name *'Dead Man's Chest'*.

The following account is the exact passage in Kingsley's novel, *At Last: A Christmas in the West Indies,* that inspired him.

> "We were crawling slowly along, in thick haze and heavy rain, having passed Sombrero unseen; and were away in a gray shoreless world of waters, looking out for Virgin Gorda; the first of those numberless isles which Columbus, so goes the tale, discovered on St. Ursula's Day, and named them after the Saint and her eleven thousand mythical virgins.
>
> Unfortunately, English buccaneers have since then, given to most of them, less poetic names. *The Dutchman's Cap, Broken Jerusalem, The Dead Man's Chest, Rum Island,* and so forth, mark a time and a race more prosaic, but still more terrible, though not one whit more wicked and brutal, than the Spanish Conquistadores.
>
> Their descendants, in the seventeenth century, smote hip and thigh with great destruction."

☞ Kingsley's story was *the seed* for Stevenson's invention, but including the phrase, *'Fifteen-Men'*, was wholly original with Stevenson.

The *Department of Land Registry* recorded the island as *Dead Chest Island*, but in the early days, the inhabitants called it *'Duchess'*. Some have remarked that the island appears to look like that of a 'dead man' lying on his back with a protruding outline of his face and flat chest. Others believed that the island resembled a coffin, hence the name *Dead Chest*.

11. The Breakers

- "There was no sound but that of the distant breakers, mounting from all around, and the chirp of countless insects in the brush. Not a man, not a sail, upon the sea; the very largeness of the view increased the sense of solitude."

☞ Standing on the plateau, under the lee of Spyglass Hill, one can often hear the roaring surf on the southern side of the island, breaking against the rocks.

12. The Map

- "The doctor opened the seals with care, and there fell out the map of an island, with latitude and longitude, soundings, names of hills and bays and inlets, and every particular that would be needed to bring a ship to a safe anchorage upon its shores."

☞ August 1750 was the date on Stevenson's treasure map. That was the same month and year that Captain Bonilla's flotilla departed Havana, Cuba, for Spain. This further supports the connection to the story of the *Nuestra Señora de Guadalupe* and the piratical events that followed: for instance, the derelict ship, laden with treasure, the mutiny, her cargo stolen by pirates, (one of whom had a wooden leg), and marooning the men on a deserted island in the West Indies!

13. The Two-Pointed Hill

- "Ben, in his long, lonely wanderings about the island, had found the skeleton—it was he that had rifled it; he had found the treasure; he had dug it up (it was the haft of his pick-axe that lay broken in the excavation.) He had carried it on his back, in many weary journeys, from the foot of the tall pine to a cave he had on the two-pointed hill at the north-east angle of the island, and there it had lain stored in safety, since two months before the arrival of the HISPANIOLA."

- "As we passed the two-pointed hill, we could see the black mouth of Ben Gunn's cave and a figure standing by it, leaning on a musket. A gentle slope ran up from the beach to the entrance of the cave. At the top, the squire met us."

- "The next morning, we fell early to work, for the transportation of this great mass of gold near a mile by land to the beach, and thence three miles by boat to the Hispaniola, was a considerable task for so small a number of workmen."

☞ Norman Island has a 'two-pointed hill' on its southern shore. My husband, Dave, and I thought we spotted a cave there and set out to prove, once and for all, if it existed.

When we tried to hike to the entrance from Bluff Bay a low-lying type of cactus that lay in wait for our vulnerable ankles to pass assaulted us, scratching and pulling at our skin.

From the sea, there appeared to be a dark precipice where a cave might be located, but once we hiked up for a closer look, it was an imaginary illusion.

There was no cave on this two-pointed hill.

The unfriendly terrain may be one of the reasons why Dave no longer accompanied me on my treasure hunting adventures!

Norman Island can be quite inhospitable sometimes.

14. The Location of the Bulk of the Treasure

- "In the captain's tottery characters these words were written, "Bulk of treasure here". Over on the back, in the same hand, was written this further information:

  1. Tall tree, Spy-glass shoulder, bearing a point
      to the N. of N.N.E.
      Skeleton Island E.S.E. and by E.
      Ten Feet

  2. The bar silver is in the north cache; you can find it by the trend of the east hummock, ten fathoms south of the back crag with the face on it.

  3. The arms are easy found in the sand-hill N. Point of North Inlet Cape, bearing E. and a quarter N.
      Signed: J.F.

"That was all; but brief as it was, to me incomprehensible, it filled the squire and Dr. Livesey with delight."

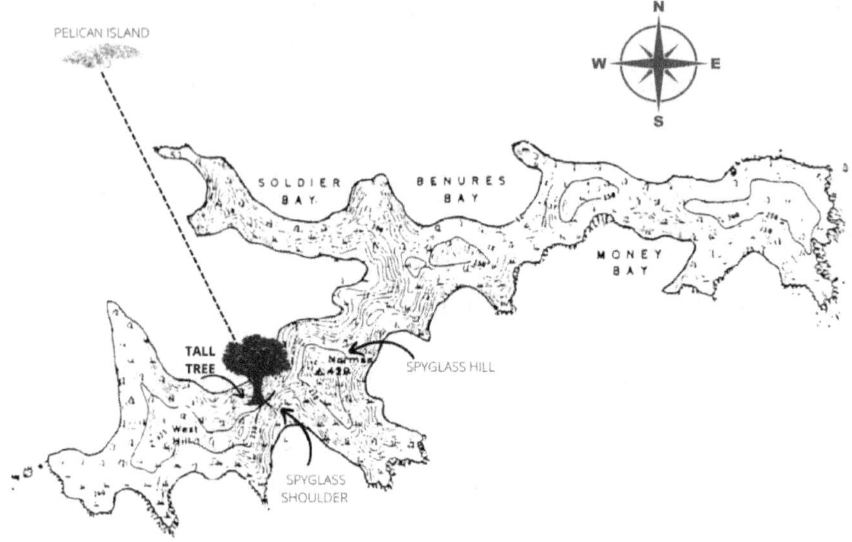

The location of the bulk of the treasure on Spyglass's shoulder mirrors an exact spot that can be found on Norman Island today.

The plateau is clearly visible from the anchorage, but you won't find *"a tall tree that rises nearly two hundred feet into the air above a clump of underwood, a giant of a vegetable, with a red column as big as a cottage."*

The height of the trees on the island fall short of 200 feet.

Furthermore, Stevenson's compass readings differ due to the orientation of his imaginary island.

Despite this, that a location can be aligned on Spyglass Hill with Pelican Island in the distance remains another undeniable similarity.

A Reputation Rightfully Earned

There are many islands in the Caribbean that share similar characteristics to Stevenson's *Treasure Island*, but very few, if any, share *all* fourteen resemblances. The similarities are quite remarkable.

Remember, not every passage in *Treasure Island* translates equally to a feature on Norman Island, so an exact comparison cannot be made.

The following paragraph for instance, describes an encounter with rattle snakes.

> *"Here and there I saw snakes, and one raised his head from a ledge of rock and hissed at me with a noise not unlike the spinning of a top."*

> *"Little did I suppose that he was a deadly enemy, and that the noise was the famous rattle."*

You won't find rattle snakes, great banks of fog, or oysters around Norman Island, because *Treasure Island* was a work of fiction.

However, the uncanny number of similarities that do ring true has rightfully earned Norman Island the reputation it has for being akin to Stevenson's imaginary island, more so than any other island in the West Indies.

Chapter 7

A Norman Island Treasure Tale

Blackbeard by Howard Pyle

When I was a young girl, my grandmother entertained my sister and I with fascinating tales of buried treasure that delighted and intrigued us.

It's perhaps where my love of family history began.

My sister, Leslie, with the author, together with our grandmother.

I remember an account she shared with us about *The Legend of El Cid.*

She told us that her mother's family were descendants of El Cid and when they emigrated from Spain many centuries ago to the island of St. Thomas, they left an enormous wealth behind.

My eyes grew wide and, in my naiveté as a child, I wondered when we could return to Spain and retrieve it.

El Cid was a Castilian knight and warlord in medieval Spain. He was a formidable military leader around 1140 AD, who became a national hero after winning several famous battles.

My grandmother's maternal great-great-grandfather was Don Manuel Victoviano Cid. He established the *Cid Bakery* on the island of St. Thomas in 1840.

Interestingly, his son helped to feed the people of St. Croix, who suffered from the effects of *The Labor Strike of 1878.*

He baked and freely distributed 100 loaves of bread every day for 26 consecutive days to help those displaced by the strike.

I found his ancestors in the Catholic baptismal records for St. Thomas dating to the early 1700s.

The *El Cid* connection was a fascinating story, and to this day, I am still researching this family, but it was her story about the treasure found at Norman Island that captivated me the most.

Valerie Creque-Mawson was a sensitive intuitive who was a walking, talking treasure-trove of information. Like Aunt Peggy, she was reticent to talk about the past, but other times, she willingly shared wonderful anecdotes about her family life growing up.

When I pleaded with her to tell me more, she recounted the following story once in the early 1970s, and never spoke of it again.

My Grandmother's Treasure Tale

One day, she said, her grandfather noticed a schooner in front of the cave that locals called, *The Bat Hole.*

Becoming suspicious, he went to inquire, but by the time he arrived, the vessel was far in the distance. When he entered the cavern, he found the remnants of what had obviously been hidden.

There, on the cave floor, strewn between the rocks, were pieces-of-eight and gold doubloons! He couldn't believe his eyes!

When they adjusted to the darkness, he looked up and noticed a huge black hole near the ceiling.

When she paused, I asked her: How did they find the location?

She told me, '*They discovered a map tucked between the pages of a book in a library in London.*'

A million more questions came to me, but that was all she willingly shared.

The Caves, Norman Island

One Tantalizing Clue

Many years later, while browsing through a nineteenth century newspaper from 1889, I was surprised to find a treasure tale that was very similar to the story she told me!

Could there be some truth to this legacy, or was my grandmother sharing an article that was published in a US newspaper 84 years prior? She certainly had no reason to misrepresent the story about her grandfather.

Searching further for answers through the locally archived newspapers led me to a cryptic clue. There was an interesting snippet published in *The Sanct Thomae Tidende* on September 11, 1880.

It read: *"Gossip has it that treasure has been found on Norman Island, one of the Virgin Group."*

However, two weeks later, *The St. Croix Avis* referred to this rumour, indicating that the discovery of a treasure trove on Norman Island was just that, a rumour and not fact (September 25, 1880).

That was all. Nothing was ever published after that brief notice to expand upon the story until nine years later when I found the interesting article in the *Nashville American Newspaper,* published in 1889.

It described how a fisherman noticed that someone had chipped away at a concealed hole in one of the caves and made a tremendous discovery. Below is a reprint of that insightful article.

Wealth Supposed
to have been Hidden in a Cave

"One morning about thirty years ago, (1859) a fisherman of one of the Virgin Islands in the West Indies arrived in Road Town, Tortola, with an interesting story.

He said a large schooner was anchored off the coast of Norman Island, one of the British Virgin Islands, and that her boats were moving along the shore.

The island being uninhabited, there could be no question of smuggling. This circumstance was so extraordinary that an expedition was at once organized to investigate.

On arrival off the point indicated by the fisherman, the schooner was, sure enough, in sight, but was already far off in the distance, making all sail to the westward.

A dim suspicion of the real facts induced the party to extend their investigations into the black hole, a deep-sea tunneled cavern extending far into the bowels of the island. It bore the reputation of having been the treasure vault of pirates in the olden days.

Tradition peopled the place with ghosts and other undesirable inhabitants, so nothing could induce the fisherman to colonize the island despite its excellent fisheries."

"The old fisherman took the exploring party to his own settlement nearby and there they were furnished with boats, torches etc. and thus equipped, they made sail once more for Norman Island.

They entered the cavern despite the protest of thousands of bats that rushed around their torches. On either side, a narrow sandy beach sloped from the perpendicular walls, leaving a channel of uniform width, in which the boat could, with difficulty, be turned.

After a search of up to half an hour or so, the explorers came to a spot where the solid wall of the cavern had recently been attacked with a pick.

The pick itself lay thrown on the pile of debris that littered the beach below.

On closer inspection, the debris was found to consist of mason work, and to have formed the walling up of a vaulted chamber sunk into the rock, about four feet square.

Scattered about among the fragments of masonry were found a few pieces of old Spanish gold and silver coin, and a jeweled sword hilt, together with a sheet of paper.

Written on the paper were explicit instructions for the finding of the vault in which it was stated that Captain Kidd and some of his companions had stored away a vast quantity of treasure.

There was nothing mysterious about the paper.

It was simply a memorandum, far more exact than grammatical in the instructions it contained, written on an ordinary sheet of foolscap paper, which was 13" by 8" in size.

Attached was said to be a chart of the island, but this was not found. As there were no means of obtaining the identity of the schooner, no action could be taken in the matter by the local government."

Capt. William Kidd

"They only knew that a long hidden piratical treasure had been carried off, so there was no room to doubt in the face of the discoveries made. As to its having been Capt. Kidd's, may of course, be questioned.

There does not appear to be any reason to doubt the assertion of the memorandum that had so truthfully guided the treasure hunters to the goal of their desires."

Flying Bats in a Deep-Sea Cavern

There were significant details in this published article that only someone would know if they were once inside the cave.

The author spoke of the volume of *'flying bats, the deep-sea tunneled cavern, and the narrow sandy beach that sloped from the perpendicular walls.'*

Could this article have some validity?

Henry Howard, the author of *Charting My Life,* published another account in which he confirmed the existence of the tool marks around the opening. His book was published in 1948.

He said he traced Fenger's moves through the British Virgins and stopped at Norman Island for a picnic one day.

After reading *The Golden Parrot*, he went to visit the cave for himself where the doubloons were reportedly found.

"I have seen the cave and examined the treasure niche, he wrote. *The tool marks left at the time were still plainly visible. The cache was located about twelve to fifteen feet above the high-water mark, safe from the most severe hurricane."*

Henry Osmond Creque, 1858 – 1915

Did Henry Osmond Creque Find Treasure in a Cave at Norman Island?

Not only did the 1889 account in the *Nashville American Newspaper* mirror the story my grandmother told me as a young girl, but it provided further details.

Could Henry have penned the article, alluding to a date much earlier than the actual discovery to keep his identity hidden? If so, then what he allegedly found were the remnants of what had been left behind, including the jeweled sword hilt mentioned by Captain Kapp.

This scenario would confirm both my grandmother's account and the captain's story, but it's difficult to know with certainty.

Following Henry's footsteps through the old newspapers and libraries around the world has been an exhilarating yet challenging experience.

For all the answers found about his alleged treasure find, there have been an equal number or more of additional questions yet unanswered.

If Henry became rich overnight and found his money in the shape of Spanish doubloons as the author, Frederic Fenger, suggested in 1917, then what did he do with the money?

His first inclination would probably have been to spend some of it, perhaps to purchase a gift for his family, or to buy something for himself to celebrate his good fortune.

As luck would have it, I might have found the answer to that question when I was looking through old property records at the *Department of Land Registry* in Tortola. That's where I stumbled upon my first exciting clue!

Carrot Bay Estate ~ 1872

There before me was a deed for *Wynn's Carrot Bay Estate*, a thirty-acre tract of land whereby Henry was the highest bidder paying thirty-three pounds sterling. Because he was a minor, his father placed his bid for him. Henry was fourteen and a half years old!

No one in the family today was aware of this early transaction, which took place on December 13, 1872.

The property once belonged to Mary Pearson Higbee and Eliza Ann Higbee, who were holding it in trust for Thomas Harrison Higbee. Unfortunately, the land was forfeited because of unpaid government taxes.

Cane Garden Bay Estate ~ 1873

The following year, when Henry was fifteen years of age, he purchased *Richmond and Ross' Cane Garden Bay* at the Marshall's Office in Tortola. It was an estate with 242 acres located on the north side of Tortola. This property once belonged to a Mrs. Riskohl. He paid five pounds, ten shillings, and five pence sterling money for the land on September 22, 1873.

Over a span of 25 years, from 1874 to 1902, Henry accumulated additional wealth by dividing and selling portions of Cane Garden Bay Estate, ranging from 2 to 10 acres.

Some of those he sold to were George Thomas, Edward Rhymer, George Frett, Robert Spark, Augustus Rhymer, Thomas Turnbull, and John Martin, to name a few.

Again, Henry was too young to bid himself, yet both of the above deeds clearly stated that, *'The lands were in trust for Henry O. Creque, and his heirs, and assigns forever.'*

Curiously, there were no other deeds in the names of his siblings, of which he had seven, five brothers and two sisters. Why would his father, a soft-spoken Christian man with a large family, purchase lands for Henry and not his sisters and brothers for two consecutive years?

It had to be that the funds for those purchases belonged to Henry. This raises the question, How does a young, 14-year-old boy from Anegada have the hard currency needed on an island where most bartered with goods?

In today's prices, the cost for the properties was insignificant, but in those days, there was very little coinage circulated on the island.

It's possible, Henry found enough copper to sell or possibly coins on the wreck of the *RMS Paramatta,* which he was rumoured to have salvaged, but why the persistent rumours about him finding treasure in a cave?

Digging deeper through the records at the *Department of Land Registry* in Tortola and the *Recorder of Deeds* office in St. Thomas, it soon became apparent that Henry continued his spending spree, opening businesses and purchasing additional lands.

His actions gave more credibility to the circulating rumours.

Emigrating to St. Thomas ~ 1876

In 1876, Henry left the British Virgin Islands at nineteen and emigrated to the island of St. Thomas to apprentice as a clerk under the tutelage of Mr. Israel Levin.

Levin was a Lithuanian trader who owned a dry goods store in town. He taught Henry everything he knew about running a successful business. By 1883, Henry opened his own establishment as a Commissioned Merchant, trading between the British, French, and Danish Islands.

Israel Levin

His father was a silent participant in the partnership which they started together with a capital of $1,100.00. John Bedford Creque contributed $578.00. Their capital is the equivalent in purchasing power of approximately $33,000.00 today, quite a significant sum!

The Great Discovery!

If Henry found a hidden cache or located the remnants of one, he may have made the brilliant discovery in 1872, years before anyone suspected.

Jill Tattersall's account mentioned the finder being a fisherman, and although it's likely Henry fished, he was not a fisherman by profession, just a lucky young teenager.

He purchased several warehouses in St. Thomas as she reported, Creque's Alley 1, 2, and 3, but that transaction occurred on April 5, 1905, two months after winning $150,000 Francs or $30,000 in the Danish lottery. He was 47 years of age. His lucky number, 22782.

There may be another big clue to solving this treasure mystery found in the form of a hand-drawn map of the US and British Virgin Islands.

The Map's Embellishments

In 1963, my grandmother commissioned Robert, or *Capitaine Tortue* as he was known, a French artist from St. Martin living in St. Thomas, to create a map of all the lands the family owned.

Depicted on the 60-year-old chart were three elements regarding her family's history.

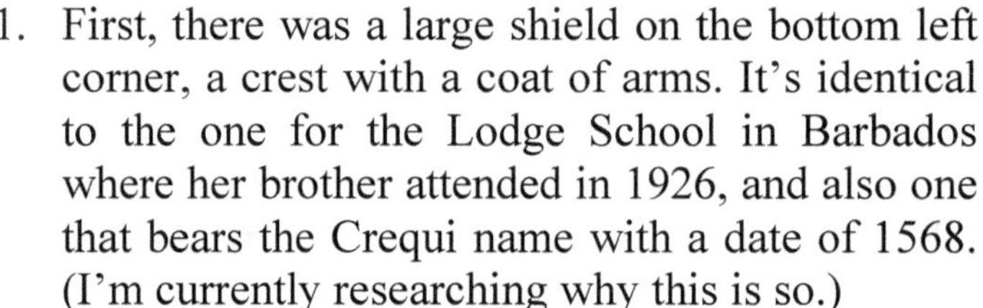

1. First, there was a large shield on the bottom left corner, a crest with a coat of arms. It's identical to the one for the Lodge School in Barbados where her brother attended in 1926, and also one that bears the Crequi name with a date of 1568. (I'm currently researching why this is so.)

2. In the center of the painting were two seventeenth century galleons under sail side by side, headed to the island of St. Thomas. [This may depict Crequi and his friend, Markoe, who left France together before the *Revocation of the Edict of Nantes,* heading for the West Indies. (1685)] See Chapter 8.

3. Third, on the far-right corner of the painting below the image of Norman Island, was a large treasure chest with a shovel, a sword, and a lantern nearby.

Robert could not have created this rendition had my grandmother not given him this specific information.

It's clearly not a map that would be offered for sale in a gallery given the unique coat of arms.

Buried Treasure
An Illustration by Howard Pyle

The Book of Pirates

By Howard Pyle

Take another look at these two embellishments from Robert's chart.

While searching for pirate imagery for this book, I chanced upon the illustration on the previous page and noticed a similarity! Can you see that Robert's treasure chest is nearly identical to Pyle's depiction?

Robert must have had access to Howard Pyle's *Book of Pirates*, (1921), before creating the adornments on his chart. It's not surprising, since Pyle was one of the most popular illustrators at the end of the 19th century.

Howard Pyle's, Captain Kidd

The pirate standing next to the family crest also bears a striking resemblance to Pyle's portrayal of Captain Kidd.

This makes me wonder; Did the artist consult the Baa Library for inspiration? If so, my grandmother must have shared her desire for a pirate and treasure chest to be added to her artwork because she wanted this part of her family's history reflected on the map.

I believe this chart is a silent testament to the secret the family has been keeping for over one hundred years!

If you'd like to see a portion of the original map, open the camera app on your phone and hold it over this QR code to scan it, and tap on the website. A page will open with a video description.

What Does All the Evidence Suggest?

Was Henry a lucky young man, or did he begin some of his businesses and purchase properties with the proceeds of what he allegedly found?

The preponderance of the evidence points to the strong likelihood that both were true. Henry was bright, and he likely found something of value. How much he found, and exactly where he found it, and what the circumstances were, we may never know, but here's the evidence we have:

12 Clues and Testimonials
that Support the Finding of a Cache

1. The oral stories handed down in the family from Peggy Creque, her children, and my grandmother, Valerie Creque-Mawson.
2. The estates Henry purchased beginning in 1872 at 14 years old.
3. The 1880 rumour that *"treasure has been found on Norman Island."*
4. The article in the US newspaper from 1889 that matched my grandmother's treasure tale (1970s).
5. The early publications by Frederic Fenger (1911), Hamilton Cochran (1937), and Jeanne P. Harman (1940s), visiting authors to the V.I.
6. The two necklaces (pieces-of-eight) given to Peggy Creque (1950s).
7. The gem-encrusted sword mentioned by Peggy's husband at the railway, confirmed by Capt. Kapp (1950s).
8. The 4-Real coin found in my grandmother's safe deposit box.
9. The 1963 map commissioned by my grandmother.
10. The following image of Henry's wife, Maria Dolores Creque, wearing what appears to be an escudo around her neck.
11. Renaming the island, *Liberty Island*, which signifies the intrinsic qualities of freedom and independence that are naturally associated with discovered wealth.
12. The 1,500 acres H.O. Creque purchased during his lifetime, including the very island where he reportedly found his fortune!

Taken in its entirety, these clues support the idea that Henry made an amazing discovery in the late nineteenth century before anyone in the community realized.

Since those with first-hand knowledge have all passed on, we have to rely on the evidence, which is substantive.

For forty years, ever since he was fourteen, Henry had been purchasing properties, from house lots to entire islands, attending auctions to get the best deals.

He died in 1915, two years before the islands were ceded to the United States and became known as the United States Virgin Islands.

What follows is an extensive list of all the properties Henry acquired during his lifetime that were recorded. His son purchased about 4,000 acres, in addition to the lands he inherited from his father.

Maria Dolores Creque, the wife of H.O. Creque
1853 – 1914

A List of Properties Henry O. Creque Purchased

In total, Henry acquired approximately 1,500 acres of lands in the Danish West Indies and in the British Virgin Islands during his lifetime. (From age 14 to 57, a span of 43 years.)

The British Virgin Islands

61A Prindsens Gade, St. Thomas Purchased in 1898	*5A Nordsiderei, Dronningens Qtr. Estate Solberg, 450 acres in 1900 $2,600.00*	*2A Snegle Gade St. Thomas in 1905*	*30 acres of Carrot Bay Estate, Tortola British Virgin Islands 1872*
29 Dronningens Gade St. Thomas in 1905 Creque's Alley #1	*30 Dronningens Gade St. Thomas in 1905 Creque's Alley #2*	*8B Orkanshullet Hassel Island 11 acres in 1910 The Creque Marine Railway*	*242 acres of Cane Garden Bay Estate, Tortola 1873*
41a Taarnebjerg, St. Thomas in 1910 Below Bluebeard's Castle	*1 Prindsensgade St. Thomas in 1910 500 Francs*	*5A Demini Tver Gade St. Thomas in 1912*	*620 acres Norman Island 1896 He paid 40 Pounds Sterling*
*10 Dronningens Gade St. Thomas **	*55B Kronprindsens Gade, St. Thomas **	*51A Kongens Gade St. Thomas **	*Britannic Hall home, Road Town, Tortola, 1904*
*24 Queens Street St. Thomas **	*14 Dronningens Gade St. Thomas **	*56A Kronprindsens Gade St. Thomas **	*2 Houses and Lots in Tortola 1912*
*22 Dronningens Gade St. Thomas **	*23 Dronningens Gade St. Thomas **	*40 King's Street, Christiansted, St. Croix (Unconfirmed)*	*63 acres of Great Harbour, Peter Island 1912 (His son added 90 acres in 1934 & 1937)*
* Unconfirmed as to Henry O. Creque or Herman O. Creque's purchase			*11 acres of Threlfall's Sea Cow's Bay, Tortola *Herman pd $850.00 ~ 1918*

A Possible Timeline

As I was reviewing Henry's property acquisitions, a potential pattern emerged that sheds light on the possible timeline for his discovery.

Henry purchased his first two estates, Carrot Bay and Cane Garden Bay, in 1872 and 1873, respectively. However, there was a significant gap of 23 years before his next purchase.

The years 1867, 1871, and 1872 saw significant hurricane damage to the maritime industry. It's possible that Henry may have had a job salvaging shipwrecks during this period, which could have financed these early acquisitions. The two estates cost him about 38 pounds sterling.

However, there's no evidence of additional property purchases in the 1880s, even though he had plenty of time to do so if he had discovered a significant amount of money in the 1870s. Instead, Henry actively acquired properties consistently from 1896 to 1912.

1880s – 1890s

During the 1880s and early 1890s, he focused on establishing and expanding his businesses, which included his partnership with his father in 1883. By 1888, he found larger premises and relocated his business from the Butcher Stall street location to renting 29 & 30 Dronningens Gade, a Main Street location he would later purchase. In 1893, he began advertising for a new establishment, *The Central Ironmongery*.

1896

Henry's third significant purchase was Norman Island. If he found a cache, it likely took place before 1896, motivating him to acquire the island.

This would give him the leisure of searching for additional treasures, while also fulfilling his dream of developing the property.

Interestingly, in 1895, Henry had an eleven-year-old son who could have been with him during a fishing or treasure-seeking expedition. There were hurricanes and dangerous weather patterns in the years 1894 and 1895, which aligned with Tattersall's story about a *"fisherman sheltering from heavy rain in one of the caves. "*

The 1889 Newspaper Article

However, the 1889 newspaper story that spoke about a suspicious schooner anchored off the coast of Norman that sailed away before anyone could make contact, matched the tale told to me by my grandmother.

The original article suggested that the discovery happened roughly 30 years prior (1859) to its publication in 1889, which is inconsistent with Henry's discovery, because he was born in 1858 and would not have been of age.

Therefore, it's more likely that the actual event may have happened around 17 years prior to the article's publication, and not 30 years prior. This scenario would align with Henry's discovery just before he purchased Carrot Bay Estate in 1872.

Remember that as early as 1880, rumours were swirling around St. Thomas that *"treasure has been found on Norman Island, one of the Virgin Group."*

No one has ever been publicly associated with the finding of treasure trove in the caves, but H.O. Creque, until 1965, when four charter guests found a small chest. (See Chapter 11)

This new timeline would corroborate the first-hand information received from both my grandmother and Captain Kapp!

Chapter 8

Purchasing Norman Island
1896

Henry Osmond Creque, 1858 – 1915

Creque's antique gold pocket watch chain was embellished with greyhound dogs, an emblem that symbolizes knightly virtues, hunting, and the aristocratic way of life. They also represent speed, strength, and loyalty.

Norman Island was a mysterious and captivating island that sat uninhabited, abandoned, and undeveloped after slavery was abolished in 1834.

Prior to emancipation, twenty-eight enslaved people once worked on a small cotton plantation when the island was owned by the Smith family, around 1799 to 1817.

Sea Island cotton was an important export in the British Virgin Islands, and in one year, about 10,000 pounds of cotton and twelve tons of cottonseed were shipped. *"Only the very best quality cotton fetched high prices because great care was necessary in producing a first-rate article."*

However, by the end of the nineteenth century, all activity had ceased. Left to decay was an extensive dwelling house, two cisterns, and outhouses that belonged to Mrs. Ann Smith, a relation of John Rogers Smith of the island of Tortola.

By a deed dated May 19, 1896, Henry Osmond Creque acquired Norman Island from Mrs. Ann Elizabeth Hill, a descendant of the Patnelli family.

He paid forty pounds sterling for the 620-acre island. Based on the Bank of England's inflation calculator, this equates to a purchasing power of over £5,000.00 or US $6,900.00 today.

Mrs. Hill was a widow without children and died intestate in 1906.

Had she not sold the island prior to her death, Norman Island would have reverted to the Crown by escheatment, like both her Pasea Hall and Fahie Hill Estates.

In order to understand Henry's desire to acquire Norman Island, it's important to recognize his passion for the sea and his desire to service the maritime industry, whether or not he uncovered a cache.

Methodist Church and Manse in Anegada © Thomas Dixon Green

A Brief History of the Creque Family

Henry's birth on the island of Anegada marked the seventh generation of the Creque (Crequi) family to be born in the British Territory.

On his baptism certificate dated September 6, 1858, his father listed his occupation as a mariner, like so many of the inhabitants.

The family's home was typical of those found in the Settlement.

Henry's father
John Bedford Creque
Born on the island of
Anegada 1832-1902

Since the area was prone to flooding, they built the house on a stone foundation with steps made of coral and rocks leading up to the front door.

Its design was very charming in the simplest of ways and conveniently located across the sandy road from the Methodist Church.

His father would soon work as the Schoolmaster, the Justice of the Peace, and later, the Methodist Minister.

Descended from Huguenots

Henry's protestant ancestors originally left France in the early 1600s to avoid persecution by the French King, Louis XIV.

By the time they emigrated, so many of their countrymen had lost their lives simply because they refused to convert to Catholicism.

One of Henry's earliest forefathers was said to be a nobleman with the high-ranking title of Count. He probably arrived on the island of St. Christopher, now known as St. Kitts, since the Caribbean Island was the first to be settled around 1623.

According to oral traditions passed down in the family,

> "A Count Crequi and his friend Markoe left France together with several followers shortly before the *Revocation of the Edict of Nantes* (1685).
>
> They sailed for the West Indies where the King's rule regarding religious beliefs was not strongly enforced.
>
> A hurricane destroyed several of their vessels; but two on board survived, Crequi himself, and Markoe, who was a native of Montpelier, in Franche-Comte.
>
> After living on various islands including Virgin Gorda, the Markoe family finally settled on the island of St. Croix, where they became subjects of Denmark.
>
> The Crequi's, however, continued up the archipelago from the island of St. Kitts to Saint Martin, settling in the French capital town of Marigot, before moving to Virgin Gorda and Anegada."

In 1682, three of Henry's ancestors, Ouelleram, Jacques, and Pierre Crequi, were documented on the King's Census in Saint Martin. (William?, James, and Peter Crequi)

The Invasion of Saint Martins ~ 1690

In 1688, King William III declared war on France. The conflict later became known as *The Nine Year's War.*

The family suddenly found themselves in danger when they learned the English planned to attack their small island home in search of supplies.

Saint Martin had a large number of cattle, which the English desperately needed to address their meat shortage.

In early 1690, Sir Timothy Thornhill led the assault, but as he was about to deliver the final blow, he saw a fleet of ships approaching on the horizon.

Du Casse

It was a squadron led by Jean-Baptist Du Casse, bringing 700 men to aid the French defenders.

Realizing they outnumbered him, Thornhill called off the attack and his men retreated to their boats.

Henry's forefathers survived this close encounter and owed their lives to Du Casse.

The First Census in the B.V.I. ~ 1716

Shortly afterwards, the family emigrated to Spanish Town, Virgin Gorda, where Francois Crequi became the Deputy Governor.

He and his children, Francis, Susannah, Peter, and Ann Crequi, lived on Great Mountain. They were all recorded on the very first census of the British Virgin Islands, taken in the year 1716.

Prickly Pear Island ~ 1724

Interestingly, Francis Crequi became the first recorded owner of the island of Prickly Pear, which he purchased in 1724.

He held the island until his death in 1729, when his heirs, Catherine, John and Francis Crequi, and executors, Philip Markoe, and John Vanterpool, sold the property to John George Esq.

Soon after, members of the family came into possession of lands in Anegada, and the Dogs, both Great Dog, and John George's Dog near Virgin Gorda.

By a Will dated March 19, 1792, Henry's 4x Great grandmother, Mrs. Frances Young-Crequi, a widow, bequeathed these lands to her daughter, Alice Crequi-Harragin, the widow of Peter Harragin, and grandchildren to share equally.

One of her grandsons, James Crequi, was Henry's paternal great-great-grandfather.

Thus, Henry was born on Anegada, in the Settlement, over two hundred years after his progenitor first arrived in the West Indies.

ANEGADA
THE DROWNED ISLAND

© Robert Schomburgk, Remarks on Anegada, 1832

Life in Anegada

Anegada was a flat coral island measuring 15 square miles, the second largest island after Tortola in the British Virgins.

During the 1700's, the family owned acres in the *Weigh Pole* and farmed cotton in the area known as *Sam Beals*. After the decline of the cotton industry, they turned to sea-based activities like salvaging ships for their survival.

William Cameron Creque
Henry's brother
1856 – 1940

The island's highest point was a mere 28-feet, making it difficult for ships to spot on the horizon. Eighteen miles of dangerous coral reefs surrounded the island, which left countless shipwrecks strewn along its perimeter.

The sad accounts filled the newspapers with the names of the unsuspecting victims caught by the low-lying reef.

Henry witnessed several vessels fall victim before he turned 18, including the schooner *Olympia*. She sank on January 24, 1873, when he was 15 years old.

His father and three brothers attempted a daring rescue, but because of squally weather, they could only listen as the screams rolled in on the evening air. Later, they learned that except for the sails and spar, the vessel sank, becoming a total loss.

William, an older brother, saved many shipwrecked sailors, transporting them to St. Thomas for a small fee on his 45-ft sloop, the *Spider*. William Christopher Varlack, a master craftsman, built the *Spider* in 1912.

The traumatic experience of this and other shipwrecks likely played a role in shaping Henry's future career.

The Dreadful Hurricane of 1867

Another tragedy, besides the shipwrecks Henry observed, may have impacted his decision to buy Norman Island.

It was the dreadful hurricane of 1867.

This catastrophe destroyed most of the sea-going vessels and created a deep desire within Henry, when he reached adulthood, to help his fellow seamen.

Developing Norman Island ~ 1896

In 1896, the British Virgin Islands economy was an important center for sugar production and relied heavily on agriculture, including the harvesting of yams, limes, onions, and more.

The colonial administrator, Nathaniel G. Cookman, who was appointed by the British Crown, governed the territory.

This was a time of economic and political change as the territory adapted to new economic realities after the end of slavery.

Henry invested in Norman Island's infrastructure with the goal of providing a valuable service to vessels traveling between Bermuda and the West India Stations.

The island's safe and convenient harbor drew passing ships because of its natural, protective bay.

There, Henry could offer crews much needed supplies and a place to rest, as well as help incoming vessels that were stranded, dismasted, or blown off course.

A New Name for Norman Island

Shortly after Norman Island's purchase, Henry 'rechristened' the island to its new name, *Liberty Island.*

This may have been done because he knew the island might have been used as an escape for the enslaved people of nearby St. John.

According to research by Nanna Wienecke and Louise Rasmussen, approximately 100 enslaved people escaped in 1840 and found their freedom in the British Virgin Islands.

> "In one instance, eleven people escaped from the Annaberg and Leinster Bay Estates and managed successfully to get to Tortola.

> They used a small barge, without drawing any attention to their plans.

> This case was of great importance because it was the first major escape from St. John involving a large group of people following the British emancipation."

> "The lack of food, exaggerated work hours and poor living conditions, and the sheer exploitation and mistreatment of the enslaved, motivated them to run."

With the guardhouses at Leinster Bay and Whistling Cay visible, they may have perceived Norman Island to the southeast as a safer alternative.

It's also possible that Henry might have been referring to the *'liberty'* or freedom he felt from *'finding his good fortune'* in a cave. His exact reasons for renaming the island are unknown.

The Naval Butchery

In the 1890s, British Navy ships passing through the Sir Francis Drake Channel would often anchor in the Virgin Gorda Sound during their West Indies cruises.

Recognizing their need for fresh meat, Henry established a commercial farm to raise steers, oxen, and goats specifically for this purpose with free delivery to the ships.

All the orders were organized ahead of time and Henry had the prices pre-approved by the British Admiralty.

Hiring Field Laborers ~ 1897

Henry's plans were moving full steam ahead with an advertisement placed in *The Bulletin* during the summer of 1897.

He wanted to hire twenty experienced 'Coolie' laborers acquainted with agriculture and the clearing of pasture lands.

The term coolie was an outdated term for a low-wage earner who was a migrant indentured laborer from the islands of British Trinidad and Tobago.

Today, the term is considered offensive.

The immigration of Indentured Indians to the Danish West Indies began around 1859. The workers came to the islands chiefly via Barbados to fill the labor shortage and had a significant impact on the region's culture and economy.

Indian Workers circa 1900

Henry preferred those speaking English or having had some prior experience working on estates on St. Croix because the island was known as *Garden of the West Indies.*

Skilled farm hands were responsible for the island's agricultural prosperity and Henry knew he was going to need all the help he could get to make his dream a reality.

It seemed like everything was finally coming together. All he had to do was wait and see if the island would produce sufficient crops. With any luck, his vision would be a success.

The Indian workers persevered and worked diligently, planting root vegetables and clearing the lands in order to provide a better life for themselves and their families.

They lived simply and saved all their money to send to their relatives back home.

Henry couldn't help but feel a wave of anticipation wash over him as he looked forward to the future of his project. He had faith that everything was going to work out, but he wasn't sure.

The Commissioner's Report ~ 1897

In an 1897 report, the Administrator of the Virgin Islands, noted the achievements Henry was accomplishing during those early years. Commissioner Nathanial G. Cookman wrote:

"A merchant from St. Thomas, to whom this island belongs, has made and is still making a very praiseworthy and determined effort to turn it into a profitable account.

He has erected a house and employs a considerable amount of labor, working up the island, which he terms *Liberty Island.*"

A Letter from Liberty Island

Proud of his accomplishments, Henry had written Commissioner Cookman, outlining his plans for the island. (October 12, 1897)

"Sir, I have erected a wooden house of three rooms upon the island and expect to have the pleasure of seeing your good self to come over to pay the island a visit. Should you be agreeable, I will let you know in due course.

I must avail you of the present moment to let you know, as *Administrator of the Virgin Islands,* what I propose doing with Liberty Island. I would be thankful for any suggestions you may have."

*A West Indian
Whistling Duck*
© Dick Daniels
(http://theworldbirds.org)

"I propose establishing a stock, poultry, and vegetable farm there with the provisionary aim of supplying the ships on the Bermuda and West India Station and to offer supplies to those on a semi-annual cruise through the islands.

I suppose you are aware that at least one of the ships calls at Liberty Island each year, only on account of its harbour.

There having been no inhabitants or other inducements to prolong the ships to stay above a few hours, now however, I will be able to offer the inducements above mentioned.

In addition, for the diversion of the officers of the ships, I will offer free game, such as wild ducks, pigeons, mountain doves, and wild goats. I will also clear the forest so that the game cannot elude the sportsman's rifle.

I look upon it likely that the ships of the British Navy may be induced to take supplies here at prices suitable to them and advantageous to me.

I have further enhanced the supplying of grass and water to the cattle.

Schooners that ply between Puerto Rico and the Windward Islands on your side of the government will have the same privileges.

When my plans are about to mature, I intend to invite, through your good self, and the government of Antigua, the Secretary of State for the Navy. "

I beg to remain, respectfully, *H.O. Creque*

Provisioning Her Royal Majesty's Ships
1898-1901

By February 1898, the boost Henry's business needed came!

The Royal Navy awarded him one of the largest provisioning contracts in the islands. Her Majesty's Training Squadron ordered fresh meats and vegetables to be delivered alongside their flagship.

This contract established Henry as a respectable merchant, a man with experience and resources to support the maritime industry.

Commodore Poe's fleet comprised the *HMS Active, HMS Volage, HMS Calypso,* and the *HMS Champion.* The *Active* and the *Volage* were the largest of the training ships, having a company of 357 men.

Henry's success had a significant impact on his relationships with his peers in St. Thomas. As a British Virgin Islander living in the Danish West Indies, some perceived him as an outsider.

Despite facing challenges and initial resistance from a few of his colleagues, Henry's unwavering drive and determination to succeed helped to earn him the respect and recognition he deserved.

Tendering the Flagship, HMS Crescent
1900

Commander Poe was happy with Henry's service and *'genially attested to this with his personal signature.'*

His approval gave Henry the confidence to write to His Excellency, Vice Admiral Sir Frederic Bedford, when he learned of a larger fleet returning to the islands.

Sir Frederic Bedford

The HMS Crescent © The Royal Collection Trust

Admiral Bedford, *The First Lord of the Admiralty,* was the Commander-in-Chief of Her British Majesty's West Indies Squadron.

'Permit me once again to tender my services in the same manner to Your Excellency's Squadron,' Henry penned.

As a powerful leader, Admiral Bedford was a capable and successful commandant with ten ships under his command.

Henry was thrilled when his request was granted!

Governor-General Carl Emil Hedemann

They agreed to meet in the Virgin Gorda Sound.

In December, Bedford's flagship *HMS Crescent* sailed first into the harbor at St. Thomas to greet Governor Hedemann before visiting the British Virgin Islands.

Hedemann was a *'kindly gentleman, simple in his taste and firm in his official conduct.'*

The harbor at St. Thomas

Upon anchoring, the *Crescent* saluted the fort to which the Battery replied. This was a sign of respect and camaraderie among shipmates that had been established over centuries of maritime tradition.

Everyone within earshot knew when a hearty welcome was given.

The *Crescent* was an extremely large first-class cruiser, built in 1892 and outfitted with 13 guns. On board were 55 officers and a crew of 632 men.

She was the first British Admiralty ship in many years to visit the island of St. Thomas and to anchor *inside* the harbor, given her immense size.

When the *Crescent* got under way, the band from the Danish Schooner, *Ingolf,* played, *"God Save the Queen"* to acknowledge her departure.

In gratitude, the *Crescent's* band played *"King Christian,"* the Danish National Anthem.

The music from both ships reverberated across the harbor where passersby took an appreciable notice.

These melodies kept residents informed of the various nationalities visiting their waters.

H.O. Creque's Proposal ~ 1900

HENRY O. CREQUE
GENERAL COMMISSION MERCHANT.

IMPORTER OF ALL KINDS OF
English, French, Bohemian & American Glassware,
Lampware, Chinaware and Earthenware,
also of
Hardware, Notions, Building Materials,
Ship Chandlery, Ship Stores, Breadstuffs, Provisions and
General House Furnishing Goods.

Paints and Oils, Wall, Printing and
Writing Papers.

Corrugated and Plain Galvanized
Iron roofing.

Particular Attention Paid to Consignments and
Prompt returns a specialty.

ESTABLISHED 1883.

No. 29 MAIN STREET.

St. Thomas, West Indies, December 8 19 00

Tender of Fresh Meats and Vegetables to the Ships of Her Britannic Majesty's N. A. & W. I. Fleet

Fresh Beef (Steers and Oxen) 7 d per ℔
Veal 8 d " "
Mutton 8 d " "

Vegetables:
Pumpkins, Halifax Potatoes, Onions } 2½ d per ℔

Delivery: alongside ship in the Virgin Gorda Sound.

N.B. Halifax Potatoes and Onions being very scarce at St. Thomas, the quantity capable of being supplied will depend on market conditions here.

Henry O Creque
Contractor to H. M. Straining Squadron

Proposal, December 8, 1900 © Creque Family Archives

Fresh Beef, Pumpkins, and Halifax Potatoes

Henry supplied fresh beef, such as steers and oxen at 7d per pound, as well as veal and mutton at 8d per pound, to the HMS *Crescent* at Virgin Gorda.

Additionally, he fulfilled his promise to deliver pumpkins, Halifax potatoes, and onions at 2.5d per pound, bringing them directly to the ship.

Henry was renowned for his reliability and exceptional service, which gave him a competitive edge over other vendors during a period of high demand and limited supply.

While delivering provisions to ships proved to be a lucrative enterprise, it was not Henry's sole ambition.

Plans for a Prospective Coaling Station ~ 1897

Part of Henry's plans included the establishment of a coaling station for the supply of coal to the larger ships passing through the Sir Francis Drake Channel.

He developed a lengthy prospectus that itemized Norman Island's attributes to attract investors. He needed help to develop the island, which had great potential, he said, but was practically *unknown.*

The following prospectus provides the reader with an insight into Norman Island's history and its development possibilities during the turn of the century.

Very little was written about Norman Island then, so finding this editorial in *The Outlook* in London was invaluable. (July 22, 1897)

Henry began by discussing the reason for the island's abandonment.

He said that "from the period of the abolition of slavery; the island was vacated by its owners on account of the prevailing notion of the time and the new regime of paid labor.

The maintenance of the cultivation of the island was impracticable as sufficient profit and was thought unlikely to accrue to justify the investments."

Supplying the Stock Farm

"Subsequent owners of the island made a stock farm of it, which was said to have been uniformly successful. The steers turned out there being equal and in certain respects superior to those produced on the island of Puerto Rico.

The rapid depletion of the white population of the group of islands by emigration, again brought about the abandonment of the island.

Despite the lapse of over sixty years from that period, there remained at least a couple of hundred acres in guinea grass, a well-known and highly nutritious tropical fodder for cattle."

The Livestock © Creque Family Archives

"This island proved that it was admirably adapted for stock farming because of its rich soil and abundant water supply for the cultivation of tropical produce."

The Bight

"The island's harbour, which was practically doubly landlocked, Henry said, afforded the safest and most commodious anchorage for vessels of the greatest possible draft.

Its shoreline had an average depth of over twenty-eight feet. This feature enhanced the value of the island in a great measure. The *British North Atlantic Squadron* calls here on its annual winter cruise, evidence that vessels find it a haven of refuge during stormy weather."

The Island's Position

"An overestimate of its value is hardly possible, particularly when it was drawn into consideration that its situation is at the extreme western terminus of the British Leeward Islands.

It is also within one hour's steaming radius of two Telegraphic Stations, which seems to have peculiarly marked the island out as a strategic point for the British Nation.

Another remarkable feature was its unique central position among the islands possessed by Great Britain in the Western Hemisphere, which must eventually put it into great prominence," he added.

For instance, it is:

- About 700 miles south of Bermuda
- About 700 miles southeast of the Bahamas
- About 700 miles east of Jamaica
- About 700 miles of northwest of British Guiana

"So that if a circle be drawn around the island at 700 miles, the diameter of the circle would be 1400 miles. (Note: *The accuracy of the miles given is in question.)*

It would embrace within its circumference all the territory possessed by Great Britain in this part of the world, (except such parts of the American Continent as British North America, British Columbia, and British Honduras), the places previously named lying on the edges of the circle and Liberty Island in its center.

As a Colonial contribution to Imperial Naval Defense, therefore, this island stands pre-eminently without a rival in the Greater and Lesser Antilles for the facility with which:

- docks and repairing shops could be constructed,
- coaling stations established, and
- ships fitted out and equipped.

Coupled with the significant fact that the station could be defended against attack from every point of the compass by practically a single gun, stamps it out as one of the likely offerings to the Mother Country, which may sooner or later be made by the Windward and Leeward Islands combined, or by Jamaica."

A Privateer's Treasure House

"Captain Kidd, the famous buccaneer, it was said, once made a descent on the island when it was inhabited by Caribs, and found the island a haven of refuge, well-adapted for the vessels of his fleet."

"Kidd exterminated the Caribs by force of arms and thereafter made it the emporium for the secretion of his illicit treasure."

"Subsequently, Captains Henry Morgan and William Phips also made use of the island for similar purposes, so that it acquired the nomenclature of the *'Privateer's Treasure House.'*"

Sir William Phips

Sir William Phips, whom Henry mentioned, was a sailor, an adventurer, and a colonial governor.

In January 1687, Phips found the wreck of the Spanish galleon, *Nuestra Señora de la Concepcion.*

It ran aground on a reef in 1641, north of the Dominican Republic.

He salvaged thirty-four tons of silver, gold, pearls, and jewels valued at £207,600.

*Sir William Phips
1651 - 1695*

An amount of £11,000 was to be his share.

Could Phips have stashed some of this treasure on Norman Island before he headed to England to share the proceeds with the Duke of Albemarle, who financed his trip, or was Henry's reference merely based on local rumours?

We might only know if coins are found that date to 1641.

The Exploits at the Bat Hole

"Many are the stories told by old inhabitants of the group of islands, as to the exploits of buccaneers at the Bat Hole, Money Bay, and other parts of the island, following the secretion of their ill-gotten treasure."

"One of the bays on the coast," Henry said, "was aptly nicknamed, Money Bay."

I find it interesting that Henry referenced '*the exploits at the Bat Hole*'. This may be another cryptic clue hinting that he had first-hand knowledge of what the buccaneers hid there.

After all, he was rumoured to have found his wealth in *the Bat Hole.*

A Garrison to Protect the British Territory

Henry continued, "The island's proximity to the Danish West India Islands, which the latter might at any moment be incorporated into the Great American Republic, further enhances its value.

In the event just noticed, it would be necessary to fortify and garrison it to protect and defend the British territory against the possible aggression of a very proximate and powerful foreign neighbor."

Types of Fish Found

"The coasts of the island abound in fish, the land-locked portion being well known to be the favorite haunts for schools of the:

- The Jack, Bonito, Yellow Tail Snapper, Grouper, Parrotfish, and the Caranx, a part of the Jack family.

There's also a variety of tropical birds that likewise hover about the island to provide game for the sportsman.

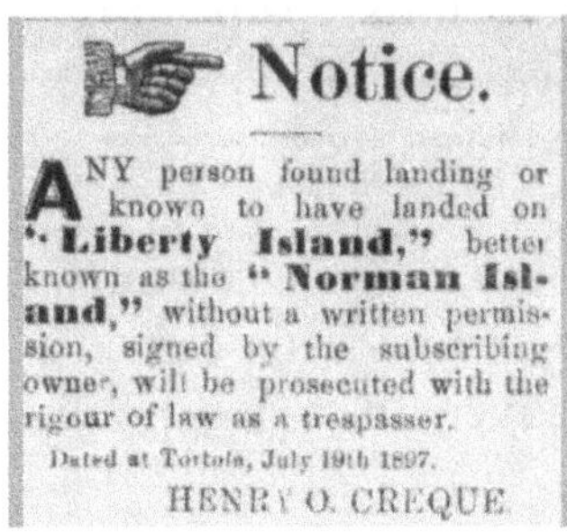

Considering the varied industries that might, with facility, be established on the island, it would adapt itself admirably for colonization.

Particularly, since the proximate markets for perishable produce are in such close touch with it."

"For instance; the towns of Charlotte Amalia, St. Thomas, and Christiansted and Frederiksted, St. Croix are a day's sail away.

Nature seems to have particularly favored this island.

I fervently hope that under its new name of *Liberty Island,* it will rapidly grow into that prominence which its geographical position demands, and its abundant and varied resources afford.

Persons coming from abroad desiring to visit the island can do so by obtaining permission from the subscriber, who will facilitate their visit in every way. Yours faithfully, *Henry O. Creque.* "

A Visionary with a Plan

This prospectus is the only surviving account of Henry's plans for Norman Island during his lifetime.

Henry was a visionary who understood the island's potential and worked tirelessly to make it a thriving hub of activity.

He was responsible for all the improvements and developments on the property after emancipation.

One of Henry's most notable endeavors was the re-establishment of a stock farm with cows, wild ducks, pigeons, mountain doves, and goats.

This endeavor allowed him to provide provisions for ships passing through the Sir Francis Drake Channel, which was a vital service in a region with heavy maritime traffic and limited resources.

In addition to this, Henry also erected a pilot house to assist captains who had been blown off course or lost their bearings. This further enhanced Norman Island's value as a stopover for ships and increased its prominence in the region.

A Treasure House

But perhaps the most intriguing aspect of Norman Island's history is the legend of buried treasure. Henry spoke of pirates using the island as a *'treasure house.'*

The caves and Money Bay on the southern shore held the keys to untold riches.

These stories have certainly added to the island's allure and made it a popular destination.

After Henry's death in 1915, Herman inherited all of his father's properties, and ever since, they have been part of a larger estate earmarked for their descendants.

After he died in 1949, the island sat dormant until 1997, when my husband and I built the *Billy Bones Beach Bar & Grill* in the Bight.

Emily and Herman O. Creque

In the 1990s, eighteen of Herman's direct descendants that were shareholders in the family corporation, decided by a unanimous vote to sell the island.

On March 31, 1999, Creque Estates Ltd. sold Norman Island for $8,000,000.00, ending the family's 103-year ownership.

Chapter 9

A Coronation Gift for King Edward VII and Queen Alexandra 1902

Queen Alexandra and King Edward VII on their Coronation Day

From Norman Island, one of the smallest islands in the British Empire, came an unexpected gift for the King and Queen of England.

At Christmas time in 1901, the publishers of a 19th century monthly periodical in the United Kingdom invited British subjects all over the world to compete for the best Coronation Ode.

Queen Victoria's eldest son, Prince Edward, was succeeding the throne, and plans for his coronation were under way.

Henry's patriotism was palpable. He never wavered from his association with the British Empire, despite the years he lived in the Danish West Indies. He joined the world-wide competition, along with some of the finest and greatest living poets in the world.

To the Poets of the Empire

They had fixed the initial date of the coronation for the 26th day of June 1902, and all poems had to be submitted by that date.

Appeals were made to all the poets overseas belonging to the *British Dominion* to bring the poetic genius of the British empire into one focus.

Where is the Laureate of the Empire?

"Where, in all our wide possessions, lives the real *Laureate of the British Empire*?", the magazine editor asked.

In the hope of finding an answer to that question, he offered, through the magazine pages of *Good Words,* for the best Coronation Ode to be submitted.

They announced a first prize of £50 in cash to the lucky winner, a second prize of £15, and a third prize, £10.

The Ode Competition

Henry gave the readers of *Lightbourn's Mail Notes* a sneak peek at his submission. (June 7, 1902)

"We had the opportunity yesterday of reading a poem intended as a tribute to His Majesty, King Edward VII, on his coronation composed by a merchant of this town, Mr. Henry O. Creque.

The composition is praiseworthy, and something of which this composer must feel proud.

It was beautifully engraved on vellum and set in an album of royal purple and placed in a polished mahogany casket.

In the center was the British Coat of Arms, artistically engraved on a silver plate. The entire work is of considerable merit.

This beautiful piece of poetry is made up neatly in book form.

I would strongly recommend all lovers of art to call at Mr. Creque's store, and if he is in his affable manner, he will be pleased to show you his work, which will be interesting to read."

1,000 Poems Submitted

The world-wide response to the editor's invitation far exceeded *Good Words'* expectations.

Over 1,000 poems were received from almost every part of the globe.

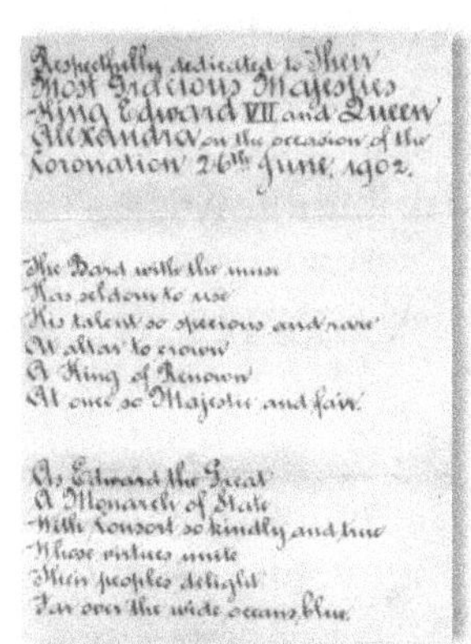

Henry's Poem

More interesting than the number of odes received was the geographical distribution of their points of origin. Scarcely any part of the British Empire, even down to the smallest island in the most remote seas, was unrepresented.

Not since 1897, the year of Queen Victoria's Diamond Jubilee, had there been so much interest in expressing an imperial sentiment.

Unwavering Loyalty to the King

Henry's poem attracted special attention from the publishers because of his unwavering loyalty to the crown, despite his faraway location.

> "Take the Ode from a native of Liberty Island, the editor wrote, not to be found, as he confesses, upon any map, as it is only about a square mile in extent, of which the writer is the owner.

> Over a population of five souls, he proudly flies the Union Jack! What a strange force is patriotism that moves this man to write an Ode on the Coronation of the King of England.

> And as fervent is he in his loyalty as any English man, and just as zealous of the birthright that lets him call Edward VII, '*My King.*'"

When the entries were divided by continents and islands, the distribution was as follows:

- Europe, 650, Asia, 40, Africa, 17, America, 156, Australia, 182, and the British Virgin Islands, 1 entry.

Examining the odes revealed two leading motives: *pride* in the Empire, and *affection* for the old country.

The Imperial Memorial for Queen Victoria ~ 1901

Henry also led the drive for the memorial fund for all British resident subjects to donate for the erection of a monument to Queen Victoria after her death.

Queen Victoria

His notice invited all those desirous of subscribing to the memorial fund to add their names to the list found at his store, *The Central Ironmongery*.

Afterwards, Henry received a warm letter of gratitude for his efforts from the Commissioner of the Virgin Islands, Edward W. Baynes.

"Dear Mr. Creque, I must write to express my grateful thanks to you for the very generous gifts from yourself and those gentlemen from whom you were kind enough to collect contributions towards the cost of the imperial memorial.

It is to be erected in London in the memory of Her Late Most Gracious Majesty, Queen Victoria.

This testimony of the feelings of devotion with which you regard the memory of her late Majesty is exceedingly gratifying and is evidence of the loving esteem in which she was held by all of you."

Today, this towering monument sits in a prominent position in front of the ornate gates of Buckingham Palace.

King Edward Coronation Medals

In anticipation of King Edward's Coronation, Henry offered British Virgin Islanders living in the Danish West Indies the ability to order Coronation medals in any quantity desired.

King Edward VII

It was his way of garnering support for the country he loved, and to take part in the joyous occasion.

His advertisement gave shoppers the ability to have the medals custom-made into various sizes with a choice of either silver, gold, or aluminum.

The Contest Winners

Within a few months, the contest winners were to be announced, and Henry was eager to hear the results.

He had spent a considerable amount of time crafting and embellishing his entry, hoping it would leave a lasting impression.

Henry's poem spoke to the fierce battle the British were engaged in that was raging in South Africa during the time of King Edward's ascension to the throne.

The conflict became known as, *The Second Boer War.*

When the prizes for the poetic entries were announced, Henry was not among the list of winners.

- First prize (£50) went to Lauchlan MacLean Watt, a Minister from Scotland. He was declared, '*The Laureate of the Empire*'.

- Second prize (£15) went to Reverend S. Cornish of Herefordshire; and,

- Third prize (£10) was divided between Lucy Eveline Smith of New Zealand, and F.H. Wood, of England.

Undaunted, the enterprising entrepreneur came up with another idea. Why not send his poem directly to the King!

A Gift for the King

Charles Levy, a friend of Henry's, was traveling on a German Steamer to London and promised him he would take the parcel to His Majesty himself.

Concerned about its presentation, Henry enclosed the accompanying letter to Mr. Fields, the Officer administering the Government of the Leeward Islands. It began:

"My Dear Mr. Fields,   June 16, 1902

Please open the parcel and examine the work.

I have the album tied with suitable ribbon, and if practicable, get your esteemed father-in-law, the Right Honorable, Sir Jessie Collins to present it to His Majesty on my behalf, or to do whatever you think best to get the matter put through.

I look upon the occasion as *the opportunity of a lifetime* and I should only be too pleased to have my view carried out, whether it is appreciated or not."

"I am a British subject, as you are aware, and own the little island called Norman Island on the chart, which I rechristened *"Liberty Island"*.

I felt that some little contribution to His Majesty from such an insignificant little spot in his Dominion might not be looked upon as altogether out of place.

I thank you in advance for whatever you may do to enhance the appearance of the parcel itself, and to get it into possession of those whose duty it would be to present it to *my King*.

I am, Mr. Fields, Yours faithfully, *Henry O. Creque"*

No Tri-Colored Ribbon

On July 22, 1902, Henry received a response from Mr. Fields. It read:

"My dear Mr. Creque,

As soon as I received your letters of June about the present for the King, I took it up to my Father-in-Law, Mr. Jesse Collings, and we all examined it. We admire it very much and think it is very nice as it is.

Mr. Collings asked us not to put on a tri-colored ribbon, as you suggested, as that would make the present look like anyone else's. It is very nice and unique as it is.

The present is now in Mr. Jesse Collings charge at the Home Office, and he will take care that it is presented to the King at the proper time.

As you are aware, the King is recovering from his illness on his yacht, and he will not be back in London for some time.

It is possible that Mr. Collings may think it wise not to have the present sent to him until the postponed Coronation takes place, which we now hope will be early in August.

Mr. Collings and all of us think the King will be much interested in receiving the present from what is one of the smallest islands in his possessions.

With very kind regards and best wishes, I am, my dear Mr. Creque, Yours faithfully, *H.C. Fields*"

The King's Response

By late July, Henry received the notice he'd been waiting for!

Lord Francis Knollys, the Private Secretary to the Sovereign, reported that, *"He submitted the poem to the King."*

This news was far better than winning the coronation contest! Henry was ecstatic to learn that His Majesty received his *"very interesting present."*

As expected, a thank-you letter soon followed.

Henry O. Creque

"Sir,

I am commanded by His Majesty, the King, to request you to convey to Mr. H.O. Creque of Norman Island in the Virgin Islands, an expression of His thanks for the poem sent by Mr. Creque for presentation to His Majesty.

I have the honour to be your obedient servant. *J Chamberlain"*

Henry's Poem ~ The Second Boer War

Henry's poem was not the conventional submission one would think appropriate for a coronation celebration. It was rather a patriotic ode in support of the British Empire as they expanded their presence overseas.

In 1899, British troops moved into South Africa, and when they did, they were met with resistance from the Boers, an Afrikaans word meaning *farmer*.

The farmers were Dutch, German and French Huguenot settlers who arrived in the Cape of Good Hope around 1652.

A bloody battle ensued when thousands of British immigrants settled near a location called *The Rand,* where a tremendous discovery of gold was made.

It resulted in tensions over who would control the gold mining industry.

In 1902, the parties signed a peace treaty that brought the British and Boers together in a strained alliance, allowing for the formation of a unified South Africa.

Sadly, the conflict lasted three years, from 1899 to 1902, in which 100,000 lives were lost.

Henry's poem spoke of the players by name that were involved in this dark and regrettable period in South Africa's history.

A Poem to the King and Queen ~ 1902

Respectfully dedicated to *Their Most Gracious Majesties,*
King Edward VII and Queen Alexandra, on the occasion of the
Coronation ~ 26th June 1902.

King Edward VII

The Bard with the muse, has seldom to use,
　His talent so specious and rare.
　At altar to crown, a King of Renown,
　At once so Majestic and fair.

As Edward the Great, a Monarch of State,
　With Consort so kindly and true.
　Whose virtues unite, their people's delight.
　Far over the wide ocean's blue.

To show to all hands, the Bulwark that stands.
Aye ready to fight and to die,
For the Empire's Crown, of Royal Renown,
And Flag of that brave battle cry.

Earl Roberts
British Commander

Where Kruger the bold, attempted to hold,
The lion at bay in his den.
But no one could withstand, the might of that "Hand",
Earl Roberts, the Hero we knew.

Whose strategic net, took Cronje and his set,
Of Burghers with insolent men.
Deporting them off, and holds them in scoff,
On Napoleon's death-bed scene.

#St. Helena.

Pieter Cronje
South African Boer General

Lord Kitchener
Victorious in South Africa

This Hero at war, sought off near and far,
The hosts of the Boer and his friends.
But leaving the few, their conduct to rue,
And serving Lord Kitchener's ends.

Who took up the role with ample control?
Of the Boredom Capitals "two,"
While 'Kruger and Steyn', and such in their line,
Did fly to the "ambushing zoo."

Martinus Steyn
Lawyer and Statesman
President of the
Orange Free State

Where rapine they make and cold-blooded take,
The lives of the natives and all,
Who helped them at first, to slake their vile thirst,
For blood from the first men to fall.

#GuerillaWarfare.

But Kitchener's scouts, have made many routs,
And hunting must go on apace,
Till justice is done, those bones in the sun,
Must Africa's veldts interlace.

If treasure and blood must flow like a flood,
For Britain's prestige and Her fame.
The work must be done, this war must be won,
To play out that "Krugerite" game.

Such "Crowning" success,
Be Britain's, ah yes,
Eve dawn of June twenty and six.
Bright gem in that Crown of Royal Renown,
The signet that peace shall affix.

Paul Kruger
The President of the
South African Republic

Though Kruger and Steyn and all in their line,
Brought mischief, and carnage, and strife,
Great Britain must still, in spite of their will,
March onward to progress and life.

The poem was signed at the bottom:

From Liberty Island, British Virgin Islands
March 1902, Majuba.
Copyright reserved by the Author.

Henry's Most Gratifying Prize

Although Henry's poetic submission did not win a place in the competition, he set his sights on a more rewarding goal.

The desire to send King Edward VII a gift from *an insignificant little spot* in his dominion, and the thank-you letter he received, proved to be his most gratifying prize.

Today's Views on Colonialism

The Coronation ode was written over a hundred and twenty years ago when British subjects held strong beliefs regarding national pride and identity.

The world today is acknowledging the harmful effects of colonialism and the long-lasting tensions and injustices resulting from this controversial period in history.

Chapter 10

Purchasing the Peter Island Bight 1912

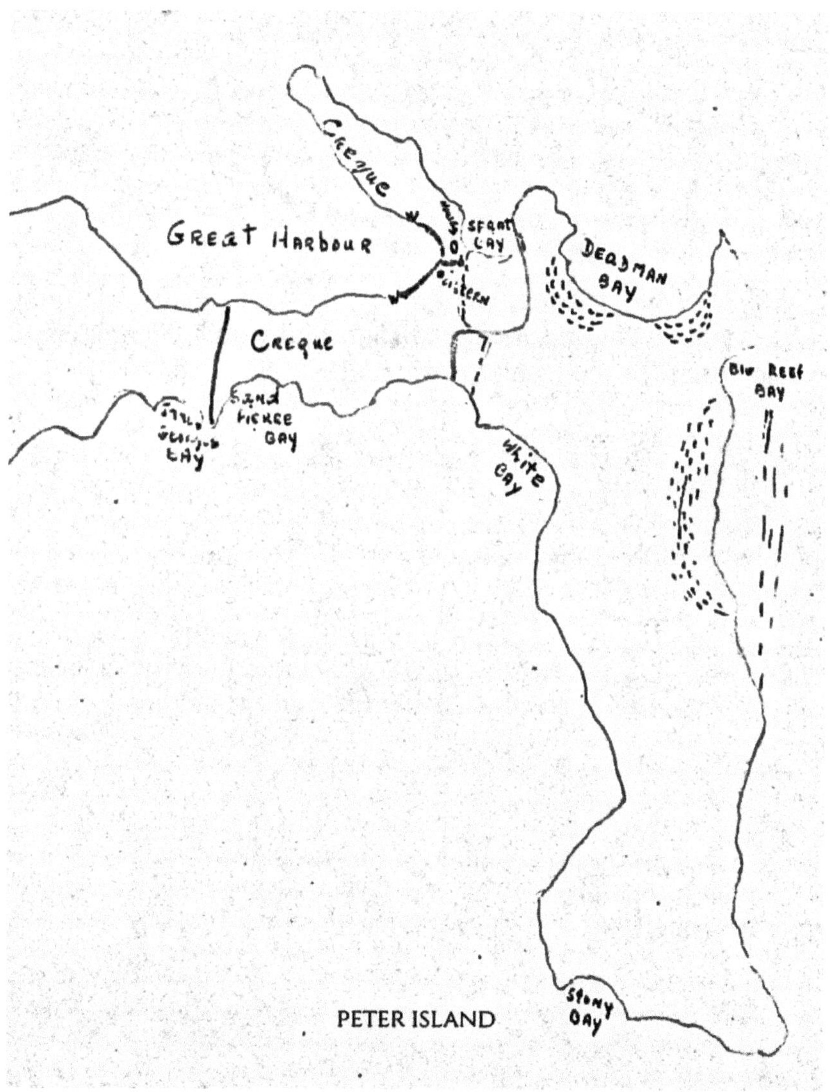

Henry O. Creque had big plans for Peter Island's development, but a series of unfortunate events plagued him.

A notice in *Lightbourn Mail Notes* read: "We understand that the old station at Peter Island, Tortola, used in 1866 by *The Royal Mail Steam Packet Company*, has been purchased."

Great Harbour was once the terminal port for the intercolonial steamers. However, after the Hurricane of 1867, which destroyed all the buildings, there was no evidence of what had been '*a fine coaling station.*'

An Idea for a Coaling Station

Sixty years after the disaster, Henry felt that the Peter Island Bight was still a viable location for coaling ships and would generate port charges and dues for the local government.

His bid in 1912 was the highest for a parcel of sixty-three acres of land in Great Harbour.

This purchase fulfilled his dream of providing a valuable service to passing ships. His total cost was $350.00 plus 14 shillings stamp tax.

The land was the returned property of the children of Isaac Farrington, who lost it through forfeiture for the nonpayment of taxes.

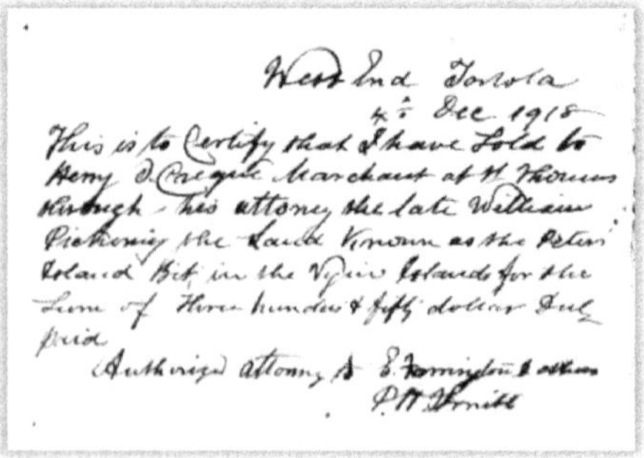

West End Tortola
4th Dec 1918
This is to Certify that I have Sold to Henry O. Creque Merchant at St Thomas through his attorney the late William Pickering the Land known as the Peter Island Bit in the Virgin Islands for the Sum of Three hundred & fifty dollars [illegible] paid
Authorized attorney [illegible]
[illegible]

A receipt acknowledging the purchase of the Peter Island Bight

(Dated 1918, 6 years after Creque's purchase)

A Peter Island Packet Station

The idea for a Packet station in the British Virgin Islands came as early as 1837, when the people of Tortola applied to the British Government to make their island a free port, and the home of the West India Mail Packets.

Although the island had virtually no trade or population, and prices for importing goods would be high, a British Royal Mail station was established. It happened in the year 1855.

The designation 'RMS,' was a mark of quality and a competitive advantage when delivering mail because it had to be on time.

Besides packages, the R.M.S. ships carried passengers and specie between Jamaica, Colon, and Europe.

There were several reasons Peter Island was chosen as a port:

- Its protected harbour afforded safer and better anchorage during the wait for the return mail than the open roadstead of St. Kitts.

- Cholera and Yellow Fever, which decimated the ship's crews, frequently struck the largest coaling station in St. Thomas, so it became apparent that another station nearby was necessary.

- In addition, steamers required from three to six days at one place to make sure their machinery was in good order and to take coals and stores.

- Rest was also important before the voyage homeward, to lessen the chance of accidents.

Some of the vessels in the RMS feet included the *Rhone*, the *Derwent,* the *Conway,* the *Mersey,* the *Solent,* and the *Atrato,* an iron paddle-wheeled steamer.

A Royal Mail Ship

The *Atrato* was the world's largest passenger ship at the time of her launch (1853) at 400 feet. Her captain in 1855 was none other than Captain Frederick Woolley, the same captain of the ill-fated *Rhone* who lost his life in the hurricane of 1867.

For the inhabitants of nearby Tortola, it was quite a source of merriment to observe these huge steamers sailing past the entrance to Road Harbour.

Remarks in the Naval and Military Record

Henry's reasons for the need to establish a coaling station at this location appeared in an interesting article in the *Naval and Military Record* in 1898.

The same reasons he gave for wanting to provide a valuable service to vessels sailing through the Sir Francis Drake Channel near Norman Island were the same for a Peter Island station.

Because of the Spanish-American War, Henry felt that Peter Island's location was *'perfect and necessary, being at the eastern door of the West Indies.'* He believed that *'the facilities in Jamaica were not enough, and Barbados and Trinidad were only fair-weather coaling stations.'*

The Agricultural Station in Tortola © The Lower Estate Museum Collection

Developing the Peter Island Bight

Henry began hiring laborers to clear the lands along the shoreline.

A synopsis appeared in *Lightbourn's Mail Notes,* which gave readers a peek at his plans (March 15, 1912):

- "The company intends to colonize Peter Island and Norman Island, and as an inducement, will parcel out Sea Island cotton lands free and provide dwellings for the colonists at from 40 to 50 cents per room."

- "The colonists will be expected to purchase their supplies from the company's canteens at which it is promised prices will be as low as at Road Town, and in many instances, as cheap as St. Thomas."

- "They will also be expected to sell their cotton to the company's ginneries at a price based on that prevailing at the Agricultural Station of Tortola."

H.M.S. Melpomene

His Honor, Leslie Jarvis and the Auditor General were curious to learn more about Henry's new development. They sailed aboard the *H.M.S. Melpomene,* which took them to see his premises on August 14, 1912.

I can only speculate that the Commissioner was impressed by what he observed since I could find no other documents.

However, the first of a series of unfortunate incidents happened the following year, which prevented the property's further development.

Henry's lands were forfeited back to the government because he too, failed to pay its taxes.

The archival records in the British Virgin Islands are full of entries documenting this controversial time in the island's history.

Families were losing their holdings because of the onerous Land Ordinances that were being strictly enforced. Luckily, Henry re-purchased the acreage when it was offered at auction again. This time, he registered the land in the name of his business, *The Caribbean Coal and Fuel Company.*

A Steamer Without Funnels!

However, by 1914, the landscape had changed and Motorships were replacing steamships.

The inhabitants of St. Thomas were the first to see such a vessel, a new ship that burned oil rather than steam.

'Here comes a steamer without funnels!' was the exclamation made when the new ship *Malakka* of the East Asiatic line made her way into port.

The absence of funnels was because a diesel motor propelled her. Oil-burning ships didn't have the familiar smokestacks found on steamships.

The *Malakka* was the first commercial Motorship of its kind seen in the islands and one of the most significant and best in her fleet.

Her profile was easily distinguishable in the harbor with four masts and a length of 400-feet, one of the largest ships to visit.

This was her maiden voyage, sailing from Copenhagen with a cargo of Italian wines and vermouth.

Unbeknownst to everyone, it would be her last cruise.

Touring a One-of-a-Kind Wonder

During her brief stay, the captain permitted a few visitors aboard for a tour.

A reporter from *Lightbourn Mail Notes* joined the boarding party and was especially impressed by the state-of-the-art technology for its day, and the impeccable condition of the crews' quarters.

The Malakka in 1914 © Hans J. Hansen

He reported that:

> *'So clean is everything on the ship that the party of ladies who, with the Governor, Christian Helweg-Larsen, and several gentlemen and other townsfolk, were courteously shown around.'*

> *'The women went all through the three decks without a speck soiling their lacy dresses!'*

When the ship departed, she sailed for the Panama Canal on her way to San Francisco, but just west of Baja, California, the vessel ran into trouble. A severe gale blew in and pushed her onto nearby rocks where she was pounded with such force that she broke completely in two!

Incredibly, the citizens in St. Thomas were one of the first and last visitors to tour such an innovative wonder.

Henry felt that the pressing need for coal would decline in the future, so he abandoned the Peter Island project.

He died in June 1915, one year after his wife, *'having been among the best-known men in the community.'* In 1916, a devastating hurricane hit the Virgin Islands and destroyed all the progress he made.

The Purchase of Additional Lands ~ 1934

In 1934, Henry's son made plans to revitalize his father's dream.

Herman purchased 26 adjacent acres to the north of his father's lands for $100.00. They once belonged to Ethelfreida Titley and were bounded on the east by the lands of Ralph Mitchell, on the west by Louis Adolph O'Neal, and on the south by the lands of Joseph Mattavous.

In 1937, he acquired another fifty-four acres in Great Harbour, described as *Balsam Hill*, bounded on the north and south by the sea. Despite these additional purchases, Herman never developed the properties.

Both father and son had big dreams for their portions of Peter Island and although they never materialized in their lifetimes, their legacies became a much-appreciated gift to their descendants.

Selling the Peter Island Bight

In 1969, a real estate company representing Norwegian clients reached out to a member of the family on St. Thomas about the possibility of acquiring their land.

The agent advised them that their clients were prepared to pay $5,000 per acre for their 150-acre parcel.

The interested parties had already purchased Sir Alan Cobham's 533 acres for approximately $1,700 per acre, and they felt that $5,000 per acre was more than fair.

However, during the negotiations, there was a serious matter that came to light that would adversely affect the sale of the family's property.

A view of Sprat Bay Great Harbour, Peter Island

Throughout the 1930s and 1940s, Herman had 'leased' the beach area in Great Harbour to Alexander Lafontaine for an annual supply of fish.

Herman knew Lafontaine from St. Thomas and hired him as an overseer in his absence. In 1937, they both worked together to make repairs to the small stone cottage on the beach at Norman Island.

Since the Peter Island property lay dormant over the years, Herman gave the LaFontaine's permission to use his land surrounding the Great Harbour beach to haul, dry, and repair their fishing nets.

The area in front of the shallow beachfront, known as *the Peter Island Bight,* was notorious for schooling sprat. All the fishermen in the British Virgin Islands used the bay for catching bait.

The LaFontaine's had a unique arrangement with Herman. They paid their rent with buckets of fish.

Long after Herman passed away in 1949, and Lafontaine passed in 1978, Herman's heirs discovered in early 1980 that Alexander's widow, Estelle, was going to claim the beachfront property for herself.

A Claim of Adverse Possession

She filed a 'caution' with the *Registrar of Lands*, claiming her *'use of the Creque family's property since 1932, without permission.'*

No-one in the family ever went over to pick up any more fish after Herman died in 1949.

Over four acres of the beautiful beachfront acreage was subsequently lost when Estelle's B.V.I. lawyer brought up the matter of *'Adverse Possession.'*

Sadly, it would not be the last time the Creque family lost acres of land through this legal principle in the law.

In 1982, *Creque Estates, Ltd.,* sold their remaining lands to the *Peter Island Hotel and Yacht Harbour Ltd.* for $750,000.00.

After seventy years, the family said goodbye to their legacy in the Peter Island Bight.

Chapter 11

Finding Treasure in the Caves!
1965

Permission to republish was granted from Baltimore Sun Media. All Rights Reserved.

As the family historian, I've been collecting and preserving memorabilia related to the history of Creque family in the Caribbean for many years.

One day, I made an incredible find!

In a stack of old family files that were slated to be discarded, a yellowing newspaper clipping caught my eye. When I unfolded it, I was surprised to find an article about the discovery of a small treasure chest in the caves.

Except for Bonilla's treasure uncovered in 1750, and the 1889 newspaper article, I've never found another documented treasure find for Norman Island before.

With *The Baltimore Sunday Sun*'s permission and the author, James Waesche, here is a reprint of the fascinating story that appeared in the publication in 1965.

A Find of Coins and Gems in a Pirates' Lair

"It all began as one of Bob van Buiten's early escapes from Baltimore winters; a warm-water cruise on a chartered yacht, this one in the Virgin Islands. Nary a thought was there of buried treasures of jewels and coins or pirate coves."

"Then Joe Flesher, a fellow Martin engineer, signed on.

Joe's been a treasure nut for twenty years," Bob sighs, "and Joe, who's looked for sunken treasure ships off Assateague Island, readily admits it."

"So, when he took aboard the sloop, *Halcyon* his sea bag, his share of the $500 charter fee and $35 for "food and booze", Joe turned this cruise, too, into a treasure hunt. "

"At first, nobody paid too much attention to his talk of galleons and gem-filled chests. Bob and his two other chosen companions, Ted Giltner and Roland Schmidt, were out for warm, steady winds, crystal waters to skin-dive, if they were lucky, some unusual coral specimens for Bob's kids.

Thus motivated, the four left Friendship Airport the last Saturday in January. It was cold--25 degrees with snow covering the ground.

Three hours later, they were in San Juan, Puerto Rico. It was 82 degrees. An hour and a half later, they were on St. Thomas, in the US Virgins."

Sailing to a Secluded Bay

"Sunday, they left Charlotte Amalie. They had mapped a rough itinerary: Sail east through the islands; stop on Tortola and Virgin Gorda; hit Norman Island on the way back."

"Norman Island," Joe mused; "that's where they found treasure in 1904."

"Through the years", he says now, I'd read a lot about that island. We knew treasure had been found there and that Robert Louis Stevenson patterned his Treasure Island on it.

It even got its name from one of those enterprising Caribbean pirates, a guy named Norman, who operated from there."

"The *Halcyon* approached uninhabited Norman Island on Friday.

The sky was darkening and the wind blowing, so they decided to anchor for the night in the Bight, off Treasure Point."

1808 Spanish Real

A Cursory Look in the Caves

"In front of them, beyond a coral reef, were three caves-three black holes in the cliff face that swallowed every wave the sea sent toward them.

The next morning, Bob and Roland went skin diving near the caves while Joe and Ted explored the island. Joe found only an abandoned water hole and the stone, ballast brick, and coral ruins of a fort, … and briars."

"Every bush on that island was mad at the world!" he says.

Bob and Roland, meanwhile, had taken a quick look through the caves. "But" he says, "we figured that everybody and his brother had searched them, so we took only a cursory look."

Joe and Ted did a better job. They chose the middle cave. "The entrance was an arch." Joe says.

"It was about 8 feet across, and between 8 and 10 feet high. You go in, and it goes back maybe 75 feet. And it was jet black.

"Bats were whirring around everywhere, and the little dinghy we were in was bobbing up and down on the swells coming in from the sea.

The Halcyon

Our eyes were so closed from the tropical sun that even with our two flashlights, it took about five minutes for us to see anything."

"As their eyes adjusted, the cave took shape around them."

The Caves at Treasure Point

"Its ceiling was 15 feet high near the entrance, but as the cave curved, the ceiling sloped down and the rocky, but smooth sides, angled in.

At its end was a little gravel beach, above which was a ledge for his search.

While Ted kept the boat from bashing against the rocks, Joe climbed onto the ledge. One of his lights died. The bats flew in a frenzy.

Back on the *Halcyon*, Bob was blowing the horn to get Joe and Ted back in time to return the yacht to St. Thomas."

" I really had the fever then," Joe says. "And I wasn't about to leave. I picked a spot. I could have gone three feet to one side or the other, but I picked that one spot."

"He moved a couple of rocks. And there it was, this Spanish emblem, all green! I realized this was a strongbox. It was something I'd been picturing for twenty years."

Finding a Coin-Filled Chest

"Ted, here it is," I said. "I guess I said it sort of matter-of-factly, because all Ted said was, uh-huh. He was still busy with the dinghy.

Then a coin fell out and tinkled down the rocks, and old Ted came to like a racehorse and we got that box out and carefully lowered it into the boat."

"The discoverers looked further around the cave they were in, then they paddled to the one where the 1904 treasure had been uncovered.

They found nothing more, so they finally started back to the *Halcyon*."

"By this time, Bob had worn the horn out," Joe says. "He was along the rail when we got back, reaching down to tie us up.

I'll never forget the expression on his face when he looked down into the dinghy. He almost went overboard.

The first thing they wanted to do when I got it aboard was to tear it open to see what was inside.

So, I put it on the middle of the table in the cabin. But the thought of opening it and finding nothing had evaporated.

After all, some coins had fallen out. So, we each got a drink and just sat there at the table and stared at it."

"The setting was wild," Bob remembers. "The wind was howling, the boat was bucking up and down, the sea and the wind banging up against that cliff."

"Finally, the moment came. Joe unloosed the rope and pried at the lock. It didn't give—but the bottom did. It dropped off!

The Royal Crown Jewels

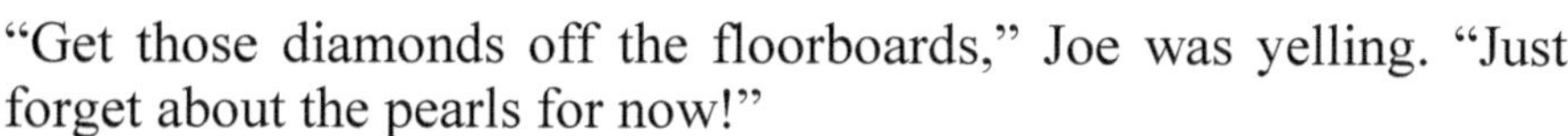

"And out poured the royal crown jewels of England," Joe says.

"All over the table, onto the floor. Those things were bouncing all over!"

"I've had my thrills in the world" Bob says, "but that was it."

"Get those diamonds off the floorboards," Joe was yelling. "Just forget about the pearls for now!"

"When the men's' initial excitement had subsided, they took inventory and found that the 9-by-6-inch leather and copper covered box contained 226 coins!"

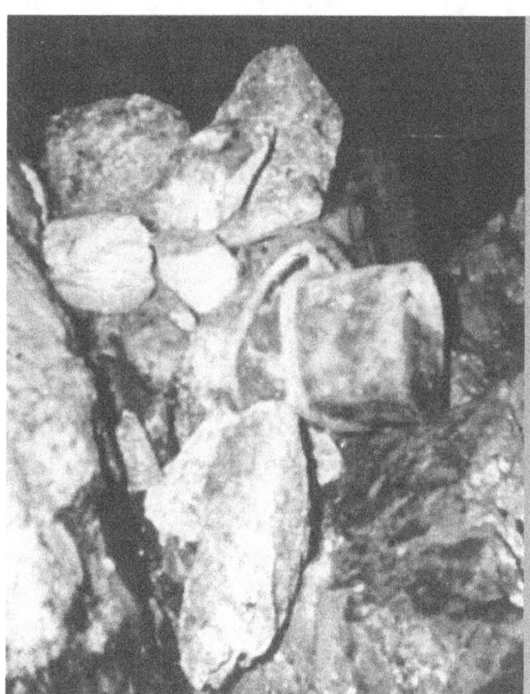

The ledge where the chest was found.

"They looked so old," Bob says, "all together in a big clump of green glop."

"There were 106 gems, a crucifix, an old leather pouch, and a fragment of a chart bearing the letters "*.... ach*".

"The coins were mostly copper, worn quite smooth, but there was a large silver one in reasonably good condition."

A Fake or a Fortune?

"The coins ranged centuries in age, from an ancient Roman piece to an English one dated in the 1830s.

Many of the copper ones have holes in them, and Joe theorizes that they may have been symbols of merit that were tied around the necks of the enslaved when they had harvested or worked their quotas."

"The stones were all shapes and all colors.

There were amethysts, turquoise, jade, moonstones.

Several of them burned like diamonds and emeralds!"

"We spent that entire night not knowing whether we had a fortune under our bunks or just junk," Bob says.

"I kept telling myself that this is the real world and that these things just don't happen, but there was that small probability that we had a quarter of a million dollars."

"They decided the next day, however, for the benefit of customs, that their 'treasure' was worthless.

"We considered the gems as glass," Joe says, "and the coins, because of their condition, as valueless. "

"We wanted to stay completely legal, but we wanted to have it out with them in Baltimore, not in San Juan."

"The booty, therefore, had to be secreted. "

1808 Spanish Real

Caught by Customs

"Joe wrapped the casket in his laundry. The crucifix he stuck in a pocket, the gems in a film box. Bob stashed the coins.

At San Juan an inspector opened and examined the belongings of the first three men, but when Joe, last inline, got before him, he opened nothing."

"He just stickered my bags and passed me on," Joe says. "But he took only two or three steps."

"Somebody tapped me on the shoulder," He says, "and I looked up into this big gold emblem. I felt like a big-time jewel smuggler."

"The tapper asked for identification, which Joe produced, then requested that he enter an office-for a "spot check".

"Seated across from another inspector, Joe was asked to empty his pockets. First came the shiny crucifix. then the film box."

 "What's in this" the inspector asked. "Just jewels," Joe answered. "Right away, he realized how that must have sounded."

"Uh, we found this treasure chest on the island," he blurted.

"That was worse. The inspector ripped into the box. An emerald bounced out, then a diamond."

"I felt smaller by the minute," He recalls. "I had declared only $6.00. I was figuring that with good behavior, 30 years might do it."

"But the inspector only took his name and address and sent him back to await his flight."

Unknown coin

Stalked by a Stranger

"While they waited, they thought how they asked themselves can we get something out of this adventure if the treasure is not treasure at all, just junk."

'Sell the story to Life magazine," someone suggested.

"Joe ran to a bank of eight empty telephone booths to call the San Juan representative. He had barely lifted the receiver when a man slipped into the booth next to him.

The stranger didn't close the door, though. Neither did he make a call. He just sat there, bending a little toward Joe's booth. Joe hung up and changed booths. So did the stranger.

By this time, Bob had noticed the goings-on, and after the third or so double shift, he hopped up and went to Joe's aid, stationing himself outside the booth and embarrassing the stranger away.

Once aboard the plane, the men's imaginations were uncontrollable. Who was the man at the phone booths?... a customs agent? a thief?

Whoever he was, he suddenly became of no importance whatsoever. Another man, across the aisle from them, diagonally behind them, was watching them over a book he was pretending to read.

Another was pacing up and down the aisle."

"Finally, he sat beside Schmidt. When Joe got up to go aft, the first man followed him. When Joe came back, the man sat down again. Those guys could have been only one of two things," Bob says. "Either they were 'Joe Customs' or they were 'Joe Strong-arm'."

"Considering the second possibility, the men decided they needed help. They called the stewardess and gave her a message. She went forward to speak to the captain."

Sharing the Semi-Precious Stones

"The captain did what he was requested. He called Friendship airport and asked that an armed guard meet the returning treasure hunters. One did, and the men, ushered into the Customs office at the airport, told their story again.

The next morning, Joe, his wife, and Bob met at the Customs House for a verdict. They knew what was going to happen when the appraiser declared, 'there's no value here to us.'"

"That was the big letdown for me." Bob says. "That was a real kick in the stomach. Still hoping, though, they took the coins to a Towson dealer. He only supported the first appraisal.

Except for the twenty-one semi-precious stones (which will be split four ways) the little box contained nothing of real value."

"It may have been a native's collection," he feels, 'or a hoax.' To discover which, he has written to authorities in the islands, and is getting a chemical analysis of the chart. As things are now though, he says, '*the mystery remains.*'"

What Became of the Treasure?

During the early 1990s, I was curious to find out what happened to all the contents in the chest, so I reached out to one of the lucky finders by telephone. He was still living in Beaufort, North Carolina.

He told me that the coins they deemed '*not very valuable*' were laminated into a handsome coffee table.

Perhaps this is where they still are today, proof that Norman Island does share her secrets, but only with a favored few.

A Find of Coins and Gems in a Pirate's Lair

The yawl Halcyon, which the four men chartered for what was to be a simple Caribbean cruise but turned into a highly exciting adventure.

Norman Island, in the Virgin Islands, where in a cave a group of Baltimore vacationers found a casket of coins and jewels.

For 4 Baltimore Men the Dream of All Treasure Hunters Came True—and with Cloak and Dagger Overtones

By James F. Waesche

IT began as one of Bob Van Buiten's yearly escapes from Baltimore winters: a warm-water cruise on a chartered yacht, this one in the Virgin Islands. Nary a thought was there of buried treasures, of jewels and coins, of pirate coves.

Then Joe Flesher, a fellow Martin engineer, signed on.

"Joe's been a treasure nut for twenty years," Bob sighs, and Joe, who's looked for sunken treasure ships off Assateague Island, readily admits it. So, when he took aboard the sloop Halcyon his sea bag, his share of the $500 charter fee and $35 for "food and booze," Joe turned this cruise, too, into a treasure hunt.

At first nobody paid too much attention to his talk of galleons and gem-filled chests. Bob and his two other chosen companions, Ted Giltner and Roland Schmidt, were out for warm, steady winds, crystal waters to skin-dive in, and, if they were lucky, some unusual coral specimens for Bob's kids.

Thus motivated, the four left Friendship Airport the last Saturday in January. It was cold—25 degrees. Snow covered the ground. Three hours later they were in San Juan, Puerto Rico. It was 82. An hour and a half later they were on St. Thomas, in the Virgins.

Sunday they left Charlotte Amalie. They had mapped a rough itinerary: Sail east through the islands; stop on Tortola and Virgin Gorda; hit Norman Island on the way back.

"Norman Island," Joe mused; "that's where they found treasure in 1904."

"Through the years," he says now, "I'd read a lot about that island. We knew treasure had been found there and that Robert Louis Stevenson patterned his 'Treasure Island' on it. It even got its name from one of those enterprising Caribbean pirates, a guy named Norman, who operated from there."

The Halcyon approached uninhabited Norman Island on Friday.

The sky was darkening and the wind blowing, so they decided to anchor for the night in a cove—the Bight—off Treasure Point. In front of them, beyond a coral reef, were three caves—three black holes in the cliff face that swallowed every wave the sea sent toward them. The next morning Bob and Roland went skin diving near the caves while Joe and Ted explored the island.

JOE found only an abandoned water hole and the stone, ballast brick, and coral ruins of a fort. And briars. "Every bush on that island was mad at the world," he says.

Bob and Roland, meanwhile, had taken a quick look through the caves. "But," he says, "we figured that everybody and his brother had searched them, so we took only a cursory look.' Joe and Ted did a better job.

They chose the middle cave. "The entrance was an arch," Joe says. "It was about 8 feet across, and between 8 and 10 feet high. You go in, and it curves around to the left. As it loops around, it goes back maybe 75 feet. And it was jet black. Bats were whirring around everywhere, and the little dinghy we were in was bobbing up and down on the swells coming in from the sea. Our eyes were so closed down from the tropical sun that even with our two flashlights it took about five minutes for us to see anything."

As their eyes adjusted, the cave began to take shape around them. Its ceiling was 15 feet high near the entrance, but as the cave curved the ceiling sloped down and the rocky but smooth sides angled in. At its end was a little gravel beach, above which was a ledge with stones piled in it. Joe chose the ledge for his search.

While Ted kept the boat from bashing against the rocks, Joe climbed the ledge. One of his lights died. The bats flew in a frenzy. Back on the Halcyon, Bob was blowing the horn in an effort to get Joe and Ted back in time to return the yacht to St. Thomas.

"But I really had the fever then," Joe says. "And I wasn't about to leave. I picked a spot. I could have gone 3 feet to one side or the other, but I picked that one spot."

He moved a couple of rocks.

"And there it was, this Spanish emblem, all green. It was obvious to me that this was a strongbox. It was something I'd been picturing for twenty years.

"'TED, here it is,' I said. I guess I said it sort of matter of factly, because all Ted said was 'Uh-huh.' He was still busy with the dink. Then a coin fell out and tinkled down the rocks, and old Ted came to like a race horse and we got that box out and carefully lowered it into the boat."

The discoverers looked further around the cave they were in, then they paddled to the one where the 1904 treasure had been uncovered. They found nothing more, so they finally started back to the Halcyon.

"By this time Bob had worn the horn out," Joe says. "He was along the rail when we got back, reaching down to tie us up. I'll never forget the expression on his face when he looked down into the dinghy. He almost went overboard.

"The first thing they wanted to do when I got it aboard was to tear it open to see what was inside. So I put it on the middle of the table in the cabin. But the thought of opening it and finding nothing had evaporated. After all, some coins had fallen out. So we each got a drink and just sat there at the table and stared at it."

"The setting was wild," Bob remembers. "The wind was howling, the boat was bucking up and down, the sea and the wind banging up against that cliff."

FINALLY the moment came. Joe unloosed the rope and pried at the lock. It didn't give—but the bottom did. It dropped off.

"And out poured the royal crown jewels of England," Joe says. "All over the table onto the floor. Those things were bouncing all over."

"I've had my thrills in the world," Bob says, "but that was it. 'Get that $15,000.00 worth of diamonds off the floorboards,' Joe was yelling. 'Just forget about the pearls for now!'"

When the men's initial excitement had subsided, they took inventory and found that the 9-by-6-inch leather and copper covered box contained: 236 coins ("They looked so old," Bob says, "all together in a big clump of green glop."), 106 gems, a crucifix, an old leather pouch, and a fragment of a chart bearing the letters ". . . ach."

The coins were mostly copper, worn quite smooth, but there was a large silver one in reasonably good condition. They ranged

Continued on Next Page

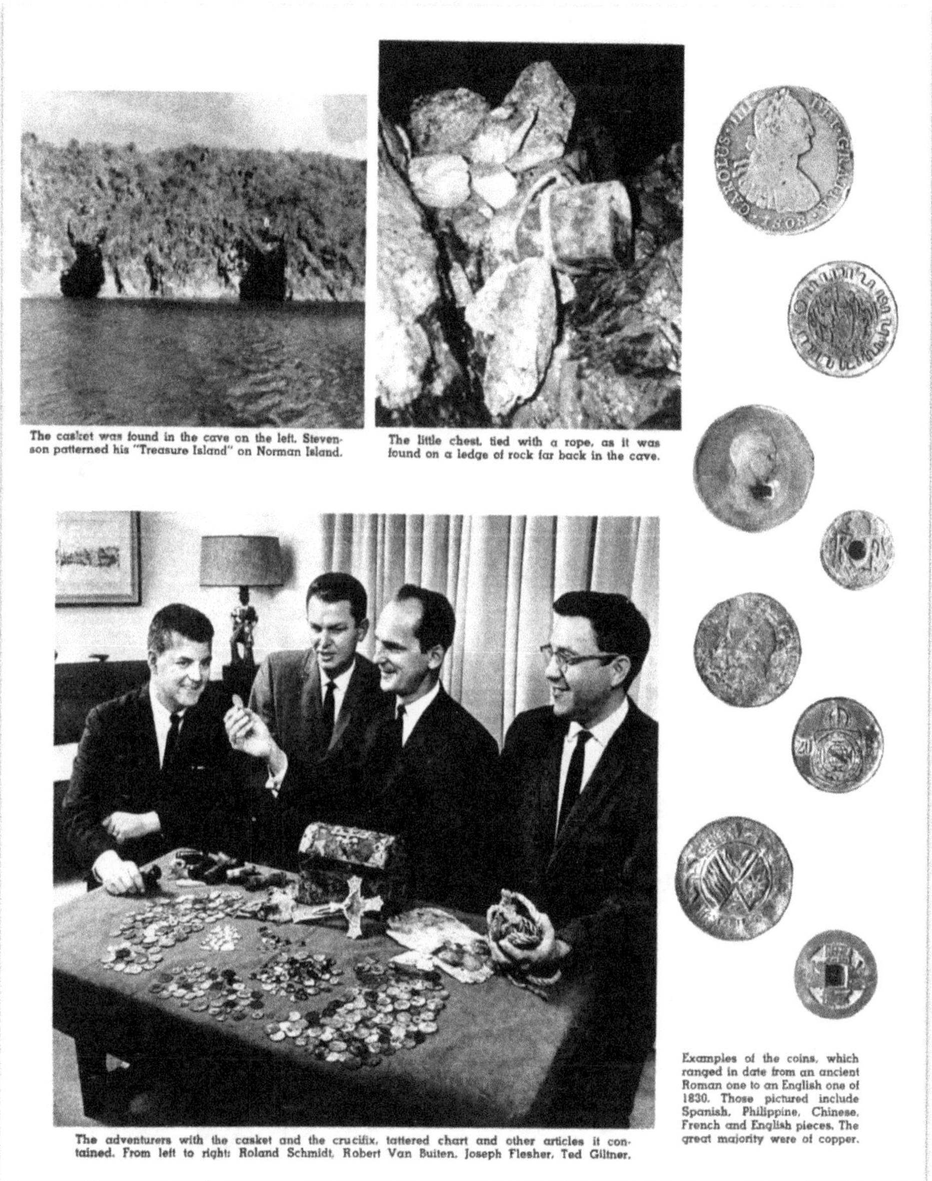

The casket was found in the cave on the left. Stevenson patterned his "Treasure Island" on Norman Island.

The little chest, tied with a rope, as it was found on a ledge of rock far back in the cave.

The adventurers with the casket and the crucifix, tattered chart and other articles it contained. From left to right: Roland Schmidt, Robert Van Buiten, Joseph Flesher, Ted Giltner.

Examples of the coins, which ranged in date from an ancient Roman one to an English one of 1830. Those pictured include Spanish, Philippine, Chinese, French and English pieces. The great majority were of copper.

Permission to republish was granted from Baltimore Sun Media. All Rights Reserved.

Chapter 12

Treasure Hunting with Tony Creque 1986

Tony Creque on Norman Island ~ 1986

Chatting about Pirate Treasure

Have you ever had a family member make you laugh just to be in their presence?

For me, it was my uncle, Anthony 'Tony' Creque. He was the youngest child of five, born in 1948 to Henry O. Creque (1912 – 1957) and his first wife, Samari Espinet.

Tony loved learning about his family's history and actively kept West Indian traditions alive for his children.

At any time, a bottle of fruit, soaking in rum, could be found on his kitchen counter for preparing his delicious Christmas fruitcake.

Tony and I had a lot in common, so it was natural for us to reminisce about the *good ole days* whenever we spent time together. We laughed often when we compared the crazy stories each of us heard growing up.

One day, while visiting mutual friends, we chatted in depth about the pirate's treasure our ancestor was rumoured to have found.

Articles and books have teased their audiences for decades with anecdotes about Henry O. Creque's (1858–1915), reported find, and Tony and I wondered if there was any truth to the stories. Other than the account my grandmother shared, and the circulating rumours in the community, we had no other concrete evidence in 1986.

I thought about my grandmother's treasure tale and how much it reminded me of Howard Carter's incredible discovery of King Tut's final resting place.

In 1922, when Carter was asked about the moment he peeked inside the tomb, on the verge of making one of the greatest archaeological finds of all time, he made the following remarks.

"At first, I could see nothing, ... but as my eyes grew accustomed to the light, details of the room within emerged..., strange animals, statues, and gold ~ *everywhere the glint of gold!"*

A Treasure Theory

Interestingly, Howard Carter found *four chambers* in the layout of the King's tomb; the antechamber, the side chamber, the burial chamber, and the treasure chamber, which was located towards the rear of the sarcophagus. Over 500 valuable objects were placed in this secret room.

I wondered, Could the cave at Norman Island be laid out in a similar manor and more pirate treasure be awaiting discovery?

It would mean that additional treasures were tucked behind a false wall at the back of the opening, a sort of treasure room behind the obvious burial chamber where the first treasure chests were found.

My mind was racing with possibilities!

Believing I was on to something, I shared these sentiments with Tony, who joined in my excitement.

Before long, we were making plans to explore the darkened recesses of the cave. Tony owned a small motorboat with an interior sleeping cabin that would be the perfect overnighter for a couple of days.

For weeks, I could hardly sleep thinking about our great expedition! I made a list of all the items we would need; food supplies, metal detector, digging equipment, etc.

The anticipation was mounting as the day approached, and before long, Tony's motorboat was packed to the brim with plenty of equipment for our adventure! The big day came, and we were off!

Heading to Spyglass Hill

We checked in to West End, Tortola to clear customs, then headed south with Spyglass Hill on the horizon as our marker.

A few minutes into the trip, though, reality set in, and I questioned my reasons for going.

The thought of spending the night on a tiny, cramped motorboat, bobbing on the ocean waves, feeling seasick and queasy, didn't seem so appealing.

During the planning stages, I was so excited, but now, a part of me wanted to forget the whole crazy idea and go back home.

I thought about Tony and all the preparations he made to get the boat ready.

I didn't want to disappoint him, so I shrugged those feelings off and watched in silence as he motored across the Sir Francis Drake Channel and into the calm Bight where we found a safe place to anchor.

It was time to put our theory to the test, whether or not I wanted to. We decided first to explore the shoreline and surrounding hills.

I gathered a few water bottles, assembled the metal detector, and waded through the shallow water to shore.

Tony anchored just off the beach, which made the dismount and beach access easy for me.

My mother enjoying the search for hidden treasure.

Finding 'Buried Treasure'

From there, we headed inland for a hike around the island to see what we could find before venturing to the caves.

I placed my Garrett headphones on my head, tuned my detector to hear a soft hum, then headed up the steep northernmost hill with Tony in tow.

The sun was scorching hot and without a hat; I was suddenly burning up. I didn't anticipate how draining the sun's rays would be. We pressed on until we reached the brow of the hill where we could find shade.

We were a few hundred feet up the embankment when suddenly, the detector buzzed so loudly that our hearts skipped a beat! Tony could hear the piercing sound from six feet away!

"Could we have found buried treasure already?" I asked Tony in disbelief.

The Author in the Bight in 1986

I dropped my bag and searched inside for my hand trowel. When I found it, I shoved it into the hardened soil and dug as fast as I could.

Tony watched over my shoulder in anticipation, curious to see what I had found.

Scoop after scoop, I hollowed through the dirt until I saw a glint of silver about ten inches below the surface! This fuelled my curiosity, and I dug even faster.

I finally dislodged the dirt-encrusted clump and handed it to Tony. He used his powerful hands and methodically cleared away the mud until, little by little, he could identify the shiny lump within.

"It's a shotgun casing!", he exclaimed.

He handed it back to me and I could see on the bottom the engraved numbers, *RG L01A271,* were clearly visible. "How exciting!"

I wondered about its age, and how long it had been buried in the earth?

Perhaps it was a spent shell from a hunting trip for goats back in the 1930s or 1940s. The island was notorious for its roaming herds of wild goats and foraging cattle.

Shotgun Shells

Tony's father, an accomplished marksman, loved to hunt, and it's possible these spent shells were from one of his rifles.

As we dug up a few more shells, my anticipation grew to new heights. I could hardly wait for the real big discovery yet to come!

Tony looked happy, and I was glad that I said nothing to him about wanting to return home. I was convinced now, more than ever, to prove our treasure theory.

We made our way back to the waiting boat, pulled up the anchor and motored over to the caves. There, we anchored in shallow water in front of the southernmost cave.

The adrenaline in my body was pumping rapidly!

I knew we were close to discovering a secret treasure that had laid hidden for hundreds of years, right under everyone's noses!

I turned to Tony to excitedly talk about our plans, but without notice, he disappeared into the cabin.

When he reappeared, he had with him an old tackle box in one hand, and a fishing pole in the other.

"What are you doing?" I asked in disbelief. *"I thought we were going to explore the cave?"*

"Oh", he said, *"I'm going to catch some fish for dinner."*

"What happened to our treasure plans?", I implored, with my hands on my hip, and a disillusioned look on my face.

"Tomorrow morning we'll look," he promised, *"but tonight we've got to eat!"*

Treasure Hunting in the Caves

It was mid-morning the next day before Tony finally awoke and was ready to put our plan into action.

The freshly caught dinner we shared the previous evening was delicious, and although I was grateful for the time together fishing, I was eager to get to work.

Crawling into the Cavern

The plan was to reach the cavern at the top of the cave and crawl inside to see if there was a false wall in the back hiding additional treasures.

To do so, we needed an extension ladder.

Thankfully, Tony brought one, so we didn't have to scale the wall with our bare feet, which I knew was impossible.

Tony then tied two life jackets from the boat around each end of a 20-foot ladder and dropped it over the side of the vessel, making a tremendous splash.

Tony laughing hysterically in the cave.

We looked at each other at that moment and laughed uncontrollably without stopping.

"Are we really doing this?" I asked.

"Yes, we are!" was his exuberant answer.

Still smiling, we grabbed our masks and snorkels and jumped into the water together, close to the half-submerged ladder.

Tony wrapped his arms around the top rung, and I supported the rear, then we swam towards the treasure cave that held our glittering dreams.

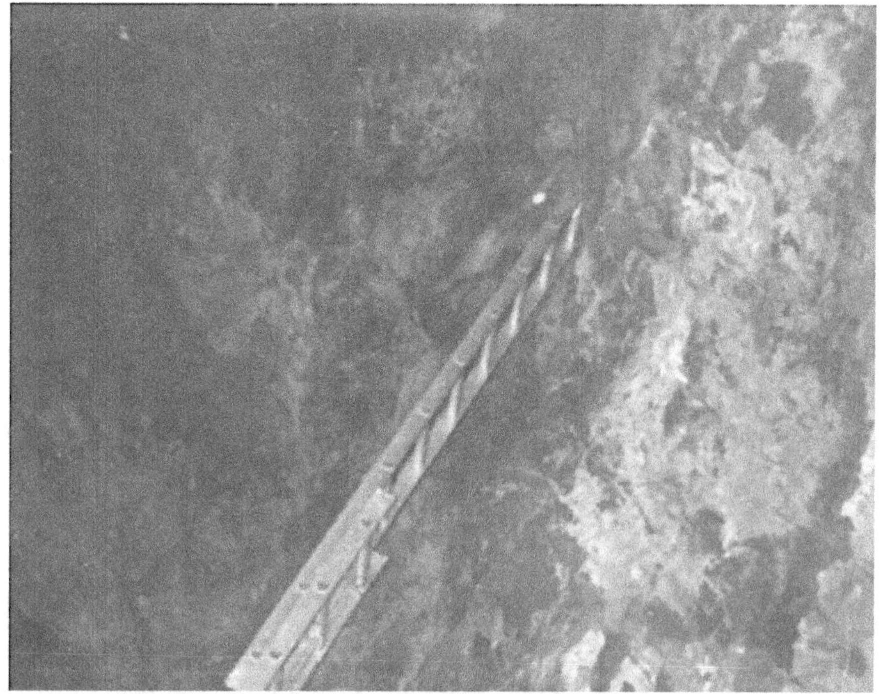

Tony on the ladder heading up to the treasure ledge with a small flashlight

We overheard several nearby snorkelers shouting to each other in Spanish and pointing at us, which made us chuckle hysterically! We must have been quite a sight, but we really didn't care.

This was the moment we dreamt about, and by sundown, we could be gazing at doubloons and pieces-of-eight, just as our ancestor might have done!

Our hearts raced even faster!

Once we neared the entrance to the cave, it took some manoeuvring to get the bulky ladder inside.

We wrestled with it and knocked about as we tried to prop it up against the jagged interior wall, but we soon discovered that at the ladder's fullest extension, it was too short to reach our destination.

Billy Bones' Legendary Treasure

Although frustrated and disappointed, we couldn't stop laughing and giggling with one another. It must have been nervous anxiety.

Who would have thought the ceiling of this cave would be so high? We certainly didn't!

Determined to prove our theory and solve this mystery once and for all, Tony climbed the rickety ladder with determination, his heart set on uncovering Billy Bones' legendary treasure.

*A British Navy button
1807-1812
Found on the Island
in 1997*

After all, the island was reputed to be the inspiration for Stevenson's *Treasure Island.*

I held my breath as I watched Tony take each precarious step until he reached the top of the ladder and could go no further. To my surprise, he continued upwards, leaving the ladder, and scaled the slippery wall even higher to reach the entrance to the open outcrop.

At the peak was a small opening, scarcely five feet across and about six feet deep and possibly two feet high. It was not a natural cave. It must have been slowly, and painstaking chiselled out of the hard volcanic rock.

Someone must have been driven beyond reason to spend the hours and days needed to create such a clever hiding place.

Given the dimensions above, we figured that sixty square feet could hide about one hundred chests if they were similar in size to those found on the wreck Mel Fisher discovered, the *Nuestra Señora de Atocha.*

Once there, Tony climbed onto the ledge and disappeared completely from view. Given his six-foot frame, I couldn't believe the opening to the cavern was that large or that deep!

Thoughts of gold and wonderful things flooded my mind as I waited for Tony to re-emerge from the hidden chamber. He seemed to linger inside forever. *"Tony"*, I shouted from below, *"What do you see?"*

Gosh, it felt like an eternity before he finally peered over the ledge and looked down at me.

With a big grin on his face, he held up a small, shiny, square-sized object. *"What is it, a diamond?"* I asked.

"No," he yelled, *"just a flash cube from an old Instamatic camera."*

When I heard his response, my heart sank.

1960s
Flash Cube

I believed that like the design of Tutankhamun's tomb,
a hidden chamber deep inside the dark precipice was the perfect place to hide smaller, more valuable treasures.

Tony descended slowly and together we swam back to the boat in silence, each gripping our end of the old ladder.

The Real Treasure

Sadly, Tony passed away in the year 2016.

As thoughts of him resurfaced, I realized that the greatest treasure we discovered over the adventurous weekend was the wonderful time we spent together. Laughing and sharing a mutual love for family history and pirate lore are special memories that will never be forgotten.

(RIP Uncle Tony. You always made me smile.)

Chapter 13

Remembering the Restaurant 1997 – 2002

Billy Bones Beach Bar and Grill, Norman Island

O pening *The Billy Bones Beach Bar* in the Bight was a crazy dream I never thought would come true!

In 1994, while living on the island of Tortola, I spent a lot of my time delving into the history of Norman Island. From my home, I could see Spyglass Hill on the horizon, a beautiful place my forefather loved.

I thought about how wonderful it would be to open a small beach bar and restaurant with a museum to showcase my family's long history on the islands.

At the time, the island was on the market and eighteen members of my extended family wanted to sell the island they inherited. Many of them lived abroad and could not enjoy its amenities.

For over 100 years, Norman Island had been lying dormant, with the only occupants being wild, scruffy goats that nibbled their way through the meandering paths.

After considering the idea for an extended period, Dave and I submitted a business application without having a clear idea of what to expect.

Valerie and Dave Sims

When we received all the necessary government approvals, it was time to make a crucial decision whether or not to proceed with the project.

The island was for sale and we could lose everything.

While many of the family members who were shareholders in the company that owned the island wanted to sell, there were several who didn't. They wanted to hold on to the legacy left to them, despite the lack of income the island generated.

The island was uninhabited, void of any structures or commercial buildings, except for a few scattered ruins and an old well.

As we weighed our options, we continued to receive encouragement from government officials and more approvals for the venture.

It seemed as though the decision had been made for us, and when every door opened, we made the fateful decision to proceed… *One that I regret.*

Reflecting on the Past

Revisiting the past has been a heart-wrenching journey for me, but it is a crucial step in telling the true story of our time on Norman Island.

When we received all the approvals and support, I was blind sighted by my emotions and built the bar on my family's land without written permission from the board.

At the time, the B.V.I. government deemed my relatives *"absentee owners"*, and they faced the possibility of losing their land due to non-compliance with the development requirement stipulated under the Alien Land Holding Act.

Despite being 'grandfathered' in over the years, the prevailing feeling in the family at the time was that their ownership status was tenuous.

By having a 'family presence' on the island, I thought it would help their situation and fulfill my own desires as the family historian to honor our ancestor's legacy. However, this decision hurt my family, for which I'm deeply sorry.

I was misguided by the idea popularized by Grace Hopper in 1982 that *"it's easier to ask for forgiveness than to ask for permission."*

I've learned this lesson the hard way and acknowledge how wrong I was to believe in this philosophy. The board members eventually offered us a lease, and we continued our operations, but it was later rescinded.

I knew that we could lose it all, but I never consciously believed this scenario would actually happen.

The island was a special part of my life. I spent countless hours hiking all through the hillsides, picnicking on the beach, and swimming in the caves with my family.

Fifteen months after we opened, the island was sold, and the new owner offered us a one-year renewable lease. This gave us hope for the future.

The following pages are about building the bar and the restaurant and highlights the memorable experiences that followed before our world came crashing down.

Here's how it all began ... *and ended.*

Choosing a Winning Name

Selecting a suitable name for the new bar proved to be a challenging task. Dave and I struggled to agree on a name at first and ultimately settled on "*Swashbucklers*." However, the name was quickly scrapped after I heard someone mispronounce it.

It wasn't until a friend of ours, Phillip Bailey, suggested "*Billy Bones*" over lunch at a pub in Road Town that we knew we had found the perfect name for our bar.

After all, our goal was to pay homage to the island's association with Robert Louis Stevenson and its historical ties to piracy in the region.

You may recall that Billy Bones was a fictional character in *Treasure Island*, a rough, gruff sailor who had possession of the treasure map in his trunk.

He was the first mate of the pirate, Captain Flint, known for his fierce temper and love of rum.

Young Jim Hawkins remembered him breaking out in this old sea song that he sang.

"Fifteen men on the dead man's chest ~

Yo-ho-ho, and a bottle of rum!

Drink and the devil had done for the rest ~

Yo-ho-ho, and a bottle of rum!"

Billy Bones under construction

Building the Bar

Construction on the bar and restaurant began on November 1st, 1997, and by December 20th, 1997, the establishment was open for business. It all happened quickly, as if by serendipity.

We hired a barge to ship all the major supplies from the main island to the out island, a distance of seven miles, while the workmen, and I traveled in our 24-ft open dinghy.

I didn't make the journey every day during the construction phase, but when I did, I was often tossed about, doused, and arrived at the island in a disheveled state with dripping wet hair.

I quickly realized that this was not an ideal solution and had to design a sea-suit.

My sea-suit

I wore rubber overalls with a hoodie, and underneath, I used a shower cap to protect my hair, goggles to keep the sea spray out of my eyes, and a life preserver in case of an emergency. Some people may have thought that I couldn't swim because I always wore my life vest when I operated the boat, but I took safety seriously.

Growing up in the US Virgin Islands, I had developed a love for sailing, scuba diving, and fishing. I had even earned my 50-ton Ocean Operator's license.

When I arrived at the island, I didn't look like a glamorous rock island entrepreneur, but when I changed out of my travel clothes, heads turned.

No one expected the drastic transformation from hazmat suit to bathing suit. Actually, there was very little time for a swim during those early years. It was all work and no play.

While uninhabited islands can be beautiful, when you have to pack and transport everything by sea, unload, and stack it all up on the other side, the charm can quickly wear off.

Beautifying the Beach

Because the appearance of the beach lacked a soft cushion of sand, various measures were taken to enhance its appearance.

Along with the restaurant provisions of 50-pound bags of carrots and cases of beer, we transported a number of baby palm trees to the island in the inflatable dinghy.

Five palm trees were planted along the front of the restaurant and the rest disbursed throughout the property to hopefully provide shade one day.

Additionally, a barge full of sand was brought in to soften the pebbly beach. However, due to the unpredictable tide, this solution didn't last long, and a significant amount of the sand washed away.

Fortunately, the following year (1998), Hurricane Georges brought an abundance of soft powdery sand to the bay, restoring the natural beauty of the beach.

Opening Day

Just before we completed the finishing touches to the building, thirsty charter guests flocked to the bar, wanting us to open early.

This was the moment we hoped for, but my first response was, *"Wait, we haven't finished painting yet!"*

"Oh, we don't care about that." they said. *"We'll draw some pictures for you and decorate the place with a few bungees and t-shirts from our boat."*

"Now, can we order a drink?" they inquired.

And just like that, we opened for business. No time for fanfare or fussing for perfection.

The pirate bar was an instant hit! Everything you could dream of that a beach bar could be, Billy Bones had it and more: super cool, specialty drinks made by fire-breathing, bottle-juggling, limbo-dancing bartenders who knew all the latest songs to play.

On the smoky grill were sizzling sweet burgers and fresh fish patties we served with spicy, spiral-shaped fries.

What else could anyone ask for on a deserted island? Right?

A free temporary tattoo

My favorite part was sharing the history of the island with curious travelers, inquisitive about this new structure in their favorite watering hole.

They were eager to learn about the island, which was the highlight for me, as I sat with guests sharing my picture book of the island's past.

Sharing Our Story

Norman Island was a popular spot among sailors since the beginning of the tourism industry, yet visitors knew very little about its history.

I created a three-ring binder with information about my family's history for guests, including the story of my great-great-grandfather's purchase of the island in 1896.

For the first time, boaters could see a photo of the man who once dreamed of providing a valuable service to the maritime industry during the 19th century, the first person to commercialize the island after the end of slavery.

Guests found the island's connection to Robert Louis Stevenson fascinating, and I could share what I learned about him from my travels to see his home in Scotland and his lodgings in Monterey, California.

When we first opened up, one guest in particular asked me with a smile, *"How long have you been here?"* "Nine days," I remember saying casually.

Then he looked at me with great big, enormous eyes in total disbelief, as if he'd found a $5.00 bill on the beach.

"Wow!," was his response. I knew then that he knew he'd discovered a really cool place.

Almost immediately, he reached into his pocket and pulled out a lucky dollar and his business card from a former life.

"I'd like to put these up," he suggested. *"Do you have a marker and a staple gun?"* *"Yes,"* I replied.

I ended up purchasing markers by the caseload because so many visitors wanted to sign their names on the ceiling.

Dave and I in pirate hats celebrating with our first guests, the Gerremo family in 1997.

I had never heard of this being a way to welcome a new business before, but it was a fun and unique way for guests to become a part of the establishment.

Pretty soon, visitors were mailing us markers and using them to create elaborate designs on our bar stools, chest freezers, bathroom walls, and any other area that was free of grainy sea salt.

It seemed to be a rite of passage that allowed them entrance to a private club. Those who were the first to discover this pirate-themed restaurant in her early days knew they were special, too.

I remember posing for a photograph with my husband wearing our paper pirate hats. We were celebrating the realization of this dream with our very first patrons who visited from Sweden.

We didn't open the bar for the revenue it might bring, but to establish a presence on our family's property and to honor my ancestor, who had purchased the island a hundred years prior.

As the family historian, having that connection fulfilled a dream like no other. When I designed our t-shirt, it reflected all the aspects that meant the most to me: the island, its' history, and its' connection to Robert Louis Stevenson.

The popular t-shirt was a hit with designs featuring dancing skeletons, snorkeling skeletons, and scuba diving skeletons, all having fun searching for hidden treasure.

Greeting Our Guests

At the head of the dock, a hand-written message welcomed our guests as they arrived, written by a creative member of our staff.

> "A Big Welcome to all you salty sea dogs and pirates from the fun-loving crew here at Billy Bones…
>
> "After safely crossing the stormy waters of the Sir Francis Drake channel, you have finally hit land.
>
> "So, enjoy a day of sun, fun, and frolicking, and remember…." *"Memories are the greatest treasures of all!"* © *Kirstie Lawton*

Twenty years later, I'm touched by how right Kirstie was. Her talents and those of our eclectic staff were legendary.

It was their combined attributes and diverse personalities that made the establishment a success.

Starting with a Skeleton Crew

In the early days, we started with a handful of hardworking employees, but there was one in particular who didn't share our same values.

Dave was in charge of staffing and one of his first hires was a Jamaican chef, whom he hoped would bring more flavor and variety to our basic beach bar menu.

She was petite in stature, yet her demeanor was deceivingly calm and unassuming. However, I soon learned that she had a fiery temper that lay hidden beneath the surface.

She arrived at the remote island restaurant every day with her personal culinary set tucked under her arm. Her tools included butchers, cleavers, choppers, carvers, and slicers, the kind of equipment you would need for a pig roast, which we never offered.

As she entered the kitchen, she would place her canvas roll on the counter and slowly unravel the parcel, as if partaking in an ancient ceremonial ritual.

All who worked under her command knew the silent statement she was making, *"Don't... mess...with... me."*
.
Well, one day… I made the mistake of "messing with her."

As I attempted to assert my authority in the kitchen, she unleashed a barrage of hurtful profanities at me. I lost the battle I was embroiled in and felt defeated. Frustrated and visibly upset, I ran outside, tears streaming down my face, searching for a remote spot where I could be alone.

I found a secluded tree and huddled there for what felt like hours, waiting for the redness in my eyes to clear and my nose to stop running. I didn't dare return to what was clearly established as *'the chef's domain.'*

As I sat under the tree, lost in my thoughts, I absentmindedly picked at a protruding nodule on one of the branches. When it wouldn't budge, I took a closer look.

It was then that I realized that my comforting friend was a Lignum vitae tree, known for producing one of the hardest and densest woods in the world!

When I glanced up at the horizon behind the restaurant, I noticed the three large mahogany trees towering in the distance. How funny, I thought to myself, that the smallest tree on the property was one of the strongest.

As I realized the wisdom in what I was thinking, I burst into laughter and more tears. At that moment, I felt small and weak, but in reality, I knew that I was strong.

When I returned to the kitchen with renewed confidence, I reclaimed my position, and was once again *'ruler of the roost.'*

Establishing Rules and Procedures

I had a fun time meeting our guests and dancing with them, creating an enjoyable atmosphere for their holiday.

However, managing the bar came with its share of daily challenges.

The constant setbacks over small matters were a source of disappointment for me, especially when they could have been prevented.

As a new business owner, I was determined to adhere to policies and procedures in order to run the business effectively. However, I quickly learned that putting these policies into practice was not always straightforward.

Despite my best efforts, some of the staff would often disregard the rules and sneak off to a nearby establishment to complain about the new procedures.

One morning, it surprised me that the overnight bartenders had taken it upon themselves to give the restaurant a new name: "VAL" CATRAZ.

The name was clever and amusing and I couldn't help but smile, but I knew that having a structured plan in place was important for the business to thrive. Unbeknownst to them, sometimes I too wanted to escape for a break.

Fun Times with the Flotillas

It's no surprise that the yachting community considers the British Virgin Islands the sailing capital of the world. With an extensive fleet of charter yachts and over fifty dispersed islands to discover, it's one of the most scenic sailing locations in the Caribbean.

At the beginning of a vacation holiday, several boats who shared the same itinerary trailed one another to the different harbours.

When the flagship of a flotilla group entered the Bight, her tall masts, bedecked with colorful flags, flapped loudly in the wind. Seeing the dressed ship reminded me of a time when majestic warships sailed these waters.

It captivated me to watch the vessel as she glided gracefully through the water, skillfully maneuvering through the mooring field with precision. I knew the party was about to begin when she anchored near the beach. The excitement and festive energy in the air were palpable!

Billy Bones hosted the Interline Regatta, the Black Boater's Summit, HIHO, the Tall Ships, the Poker Run, as well as the Moorings and Sunsail flotillas, to name a few.

When the sailors came ashore, their exuberance and fun spirit added to the festive atmosphere.

We set the dinner tables up in advance for each vessel, but many times, upwards of 30+ people chose to sit at one long table.

Providing hot meals simultaneously for all of our guests was a challenging task, and the kitchen's ability to rise to the occasion constantly impressed me.

As an added touch, I distributed pirate hats to each guest as a way of expressing my appreciation for their patronage.

To my surprise, this small gesture of gratitude had a significant impact. Almost immediately, patrons would grab their cameras to snap a group photo with their new hats.

Seeing these images later brought back fond memories that I treasure today.

A Happy Hour Blast

Every day at 5pm, we kicked off happy hour with a loud blast from an antique brass cannon, a gift from the captain of one of the Tall Ships.

This was our signature announcement, a cue for many of the vacationers to come and join us for drinks before the sun set.

As soon as they arrived, a large batch of our popular specialty drink, *The Billy Bones Pirate's Punch,* awaited them at the bar.

This was a unique blend of Caribbean juices, spiced rum, and a generous amount of grated nutmeg.

We garnished each drink with a small skeleton toy that looked like it was crawling out of the cup, a fun souvenir for those who tried it.

Valerie Sims at Billy Bones ~ © Julian Putley

For every five drinks ordered, the sixth one was free, making it a perfect option for sharing among a group of friends.

This drink was a hit among the boaters and contributed to the party atmosphere.

Just before the sun dipped behind the island of St. John, the crowd would gather to watch the sky light up with a spectacular display of colors.

Crimson red, deep orange, and yellow clouds burst across the horizon, creating a silent fireworks display.

The ever-changing colors, combined with the rhythmic music playing in the background, marked the end of each magical day.

At dusk, the beach crowd filled the tables.

The Restaurant's Specialty

The dinner guests raved about our BBQ Baby-back ribs, which gained us a reputation for mouth-watering meat that melted off the bone. The sauce was tasty too and should have been bottled.

One day, I asked our new chef how she made the ribs so consistently delicious. Carol simply replied, "*I prepare all my food with love.*"

I had never considered that as a factor in cooking, but I couldn't deny the truth in her words. Everything Carol prepared was absolutely scrumptious!

Cooking for a Hungry Crew

Even the process of making fresh bread from scratch was a treat.

Watching Carol knead the dough, and then leave it to rise on the counter, encouraged the staff to line up for a sample as soon as it came out of the oven, piping hot.

Carol couldn't bake the loaves fast enough to keep up with the demand from both the restaurant and the hungry crew.

Our conch fritters and fish bites were also a hit, and the Spanish girls in the kitchen added so much flavor and flair to them as well as to the overall atmosphere.

Despite the language barrier, we used hand gestures to communicate when we couldn't understand each other.

The kitchen can be a stressful place, working under constant pressure. When a staff member didn't show up for work, everyone else had to work that much harder.

Sometime the tension in the kitchen exceeded my expectations, and I lost my temper. I don't use profanities, so I made up my own.

The staff knew when I muttered *"Koramina-Solamina"* under my breath, I was angry. The words had no meaning and didn't exist in any language, but its emphasis, combined with my facial expressions, spoke volumes.

Once the atmosphere returned to normal, everyone was relieved and happy again, aware that the tense moments were behind us, and we were still a family.

Working in an off-island kitchen was challenging, but when the compliments rolled in, the stress was worth all the effort.

Dancing After Dinner

As the night progressed, the bartenders gradually amped up the music's tempo, encouraging the guests to migrate towards the dance floor. This was my favorite part of the evening!

When Kidd, one of our bartenders, played popular songs such as *Macarena* or the *Electric Slide*, I couldn't help but join in the fun.

The dance floor was an open wooden platform where the light from the moon created moving shadows behind me, a silent dance partner that mimicked my moves.

The warmth of the evening, along with the upbeat music and the sense of camaraderie, created a truly magical atmosphere. Dancing under a starry sky, surrounded by happy revelers, was an unforgettable experience that filled me with joy.

After all the closing chores were done, the staff and I made the seven-mile trek across the dark channel back to our home base on Tortola, all thanks to Captain Everton.

The Pirate's Plunder Gift Shop

Of all my responsibilities at the restaurant, the *Pirate's Plunder Gift Shop* was my favorite endeavor because it was a place I could be the most creative.

I remember wanting the design to have that cave-like feel, with pirate-themed merchandise on display throughout. We painted the walls gray and used chicken wire to create the shape of the cave's curves.

Our T-Shirt design

One of the most popular items at the store was the Billy Bones' t-shirt. It featured a design with dancing skeletons on the beach and the words *Billy Bones* written above.

Sandra Vassell

These shirts were a hit with customers of all ages. The store also offered a wide range of other pirate-themed items, such as hats, caps, shot glasses, books, flags, and more.

Sandra, our first gift shop attendant, had a radiant smile that brightened everyone's day and lit up the shop.

The Pirate-Themed Parties

The uninhabited island was the perfect place to host a variety of fun-filled activities for boaters who came ashore. We welcomed everyone to our pirate paradise.

Besides dancing, we offered everything from Halloween costume parties and treasure hunts to crab races and New Year's Eve bashes.

The Spooktacular Halloween Parties

The Halloween parties were our favorite, a truly spooktacular event! Advertisements promised prizes to the '*most wickedly frolicsome, bewitching, and bewildering costume,*' in the competition.

"But beware," it said, "tis the night for bad behavior, so prepare to put a few more skeletons in that closet!"

The atmosphere was electric, with decorations that included skeletons, spiders, and skull cups for a popular rum-blended cocktail. I loved shopping for all the theme-based decorations that added to the party atmosphere.

Guests arrived dressed in a wide variety of costumes, from witches and vampires to superheroes and movie characters. They were imaginative and creative, and it was so much fun to see everyone's unique take on the holiday, knowing they had limited supplies on their boats.

The specialty drinks were a hit too, with the bartenders working hard to keep up with the demand for their spooky creations.

As the night went on, guests moved to the beach to shimmy and shake to the rhythmic music until the wee hours of the morning.

Occasionally, a conga line would form, and participants would dance in a snaking formation, weaving in and out of the tables.

The energy was infectious, as the line moved to the beat of the music, swaying, and twisting in time with the rhythm.

Andy, Rachel, Randy, Kidd, and Kevin at Billy Bones Beach Bar

Our Limbo-Dancing Bartender

The highlight of the evening was our limbo-dancing bartender, who performed for the cheering crowd.

Randy was known for his ability to go lower than anyone else, and he always left the crowds amazed by his flexibility and grace, as well as his agility and skill.

The guests were mesmerized by the way he effortlessly slipped under the limbo pole with ease when it was inches off the ground.

He seemed to defy gravity as he went lower and lower, his body gliding smoothly past the pole without touching it or falling.

Randy was a true showman, and he knew how to keep everyone engaged and entertained.

His unique combination of bartending and limbo dancing made him a one-of-a-kind entertainer, and he was not the only talented member of the team.

Fire Breathing on the Beach

Ian, another gifted bartender, lit up the beach with his fire breathing skills, mesmerizing the crowd.

Armed with a bottle of high-proof alcohol and a torch, Ian began his routine by blowing fire to the beat of the music.

He had an incredible sense of timing and knew just when to unleash a burst of fire by spitting alcohol on the torch. Sometimes he appeared to swallow the engulfed stick, creating a truly memorable experience. But Ian's skills weren't just limited to fire breathing.

He had a great sense of showmanship, like Randy, and knew how to keep the crowd on the edge of their seats. Ian's performances always left his admirers on the beach wanting more.

The Treasure Hunts

The treasure hunts on the island were an exciting adventure that I organized in advance for large groups.

The hunt was based on a crossword puzzle that participants had to solve in order to find the location of the treasure. It was such fun!

Marlene and Bob Malacarne
My biggest fans

The puzzle was filled with clues and riddles that led participants scurrying to different parts of the island.

The clues became increasingly difficult as the participants progressed through the treasure hunt and required a lot of thinking and problem-solving skills, but the ultimate prize was worth their participation.

The Crab Races

Crab racing was a thrilling way we added excitement for the large groups who visited us during the day, like the Windjammer Barefoot Cruises.

The tall ship schooner, *S/V Flying Cloud* was a frequent visitor to our shores.

She was originally a 200-foot cadet training ship built for the French Navy.

Her crew introduced us to this fun activity by bringing a bucket of soldier crabs ashore, numbering them, and allowing guests to place bets on their favorite crab before the race began.

I drew a circle with chalk on the restaurant floor, and the first crab to exit the circle and cross the finish line was declared the winner.

As the crabs scurried towards the finish, the excitement was palpable as everyone cheered for their chosen crab.

The races were usually brief, but the thrill of watching these tiny creatures race to the finish was undeniable.

The unpredictability of the crabs made it difficult to know who would win, especially when one or more crabs were slow or stopped altogether, adding to the excitement.

Watching the enjoyment everyone had made the days seem more like fun, than work, ... *just like the New Year's Eve parties.*

Pirate party guests

The Millennial New Year's Eve Bash

The Millennial New Year's Eve party in 2000 was legendary, with sparklers, music, and delicious food.

Despite the sense of excitement the new year brought, it was also a time of uncertainty.

In the lead up to the new year, there was widespread fear and concern that the world would end because of the so-called Millennium Bug or Y2K Bug.

This was a computer glitch that was thought to occur as a result of software that used only two digits to represent the year.

This meant that at the turn of the millennium, computers would interpret the year as 00 and could malfunction or shut down.

Many people feared that this would cause widespread chaos and catastrophic events.

Bartenders: Kidd, and April

But as the clock struck midnight at Billy Bones, the crowd erupted into cheers and welcomed the new millennium.

No one seemed to care about the Millennium Bug!

Everyone was in high spirits and dressed in their wildest pirate party attire.

The music was loud and upbeat, with the DJ playing all the popular hits from the 1990s.

Dancing songs like *Believe* by Cher, *Livin la Vida Loca* by Ricky Martin, and *Baby One More Time* by Britney Spears were popular.

He also blasted hot Reggae tracks, and Calypso hits from the Mighty Sparrow, the King of Calypso.

Interestingly, there was one artist the bartenders refused to play when his music was requested. It was Jimmy Buffett.

Anyone who asked to play his tracks would have to double the tip jar, an insider joke the bartenders had with each other.

Late into the evening, the drinks were still flowing, and both the dance floor and the beach were packed with people dancing and singing along to the music.

With the world not ending as predicted, the partygoers were free to let loose and enjoy themselves with no worries.

Dave and I closed the party with feelings of hope and optimism for the future, not knowing that the fun times would come to an end in two short years.

Leaving the Bight for the last time ~ March 31, 2002

The Black Spot ~ Closing the Bar

In February 1999, we were informed that the island had been sold, and a contract signed, leaving us facing an uncertain future.

The day I had been dreading came when *the unthinkable happened.* On March 31, 2002, *The Billy Bones Beach Bar and Grill* was forced to close its doors for good.

Reflecting back, I realized that Robert Louis Stevenson spoke of the death of Billy Bones, his fictional character, and how he died. It may have been a foreshadowing for the business' demise.

If I had paid closer attention to that foreboding chapter in his novel, perhaps I could have prepared myself, but I didn't.

In *Treasure Island,* Billy Bones collapsed after he received a little round paper that was black on the one side. It was the notorious 'black spot,' the mark of imminent death among pirate crews. There was a cryptic message written on the other side, in a very good, clear hand. It warned: *"You have till ten tonight."*

For the little bar we loved so much, that began out of a love for our family's history, our legal notice effectively warned us of the same fate. '*We had till the end of the month.*'

Just as the bar started, without fuss or fanfare, it ended with five years of fun and magical memories. I couldn't help but feel grateful for all the experiences and good times the beach bar had given me.

My Last Tokens of Love

I spent the last moments photographing all the marker-drawn memories on the ceiling and removed all the stapled souvenirs, calling cards, t-shirts, and currency from every country as a reminder of the good times we had.

My mother came over from St. John and helped me paint over the graffiti after the souvenirs were removed.

I snapped a parting photo of the last patrons to visit our pirate bar, regretting that I never had time to find out where they were from, or to share a little island history with them.

As a final task, I raked the perimeter of the building to leave the sand clean of debris. I then gave the guard, stationed on the island, the keys to the restroom so that he didn't have to break in to gain access.

They were hanging on a mahogany keychain shaped like a key.

These gestures were my last tokens of love for the place that Dave and I had built and loved.

Our lasts guests ~ March 31, 2002

A Bittersweet Moment

Just before I walked down the concrete path, *for the final time,* the chef stopped me by tapping on my shoulder.

Carol reached for my hand and poured a handful of salt into my palm and said, *"Val, throw this over your shoulder and never look back."*

It was a bittersweet moment, but I followed her instruction, knowing that this chapter of my life had come to an end.

I couldn't help but think of all the ups and downs, the laughter, and tears, and all the wonderful people I had met and worked with along the way.

As we slowly motored out of the harbour with our pirate flag flying high off the stern, I did glance back one last time, but only to take a final photograph of our beloved restaurant.

When I turned my head, the name of one of the vessels anchored near the mouth of the bay caught my eye.

It was called *Gallant Lady,* an elegant name for a boat, implying grace and bravery.

Seeing it gave me renewed hope and strength in knowing that everything was going to be alright.

A Logbook of Memories

Below are a few memorable comments from our early years. They were captured in a logbook we kept when the restaurant first opened more than two decades ago.

Jan 24, 1998
Valerie, on this our 15th trip to the BVI's, we have made a marvelous new discovery – your *"Billy Bones"*.

Thanks for sharing with us your memory book of the Creque family and associated articles. They were informative and fascinating. Obviously, you will be successful. Indeed, you already are!

And you serve the thickest cheeseburgers I've ever had in my life!!

With your extra friendly demeanor to all guests, your future is guaranteed.

Best of luck and health through an extended future. Like General MacArthur said, *"We Shall Return!" ~ Dick, Aiken, and Shirley, Cape Cod, Mass, USA.*

Jan 3, 1998
What a great paradise you've created on Norman Island! Best of luck to you. We've been coming here for 17 years, and Norman Island has a special meaning to us and a special place in our hearts!"

Here's to you finding the buried treasure! *~ Sea Lark, Dan and Karen, Madison, WI USA*

Jan 7, 1998
To Valerie, David with Staff!
We have been looking for the treasure all over the BVI and finally we found it *–Billy Bones—*
Thanks for your great hospitality! We will be back! Once more!
We wish you good luck in the future! Lot of love

<u>Jan 9, 1998</u>
Valerie, Best wishes for success with your dream.
The food, atmosphere and friendship were outstanding. *JR ~ Capt. and owner, Richmond, Indiana.*

<u>Jan 10, 1998</u>
What a wonderful experience! You made us feel special!
Good luck to you, *~ Ron and Marian, Oregon*

<u>Jan 11, 1998</u>
Three times here in 3 weeks. I guess it hits the spot.
Great Painkillers, music, and nice people! Be back again, best of luck. *~ Captain Tom*

<u>Jan 13, 1998</u>
Many thanks for an excellent meal, a perfect hostess in this most beautiful place. May you go forward to a great and long success as we hope to be back many times to say thank you for another perfect time. *~ Anthony*

<u>Jan 13, 1998</u>
Best of luck on the treasure hunt! You have one here at Billy Bones already. Good food! Good atmosphere. *~ Kelly and Deb*

<u>Jan 2, 2001</u>
Hello Valerie! Back for my 10th time with another family group on my boat, the *Payback*. Hope you enjoyed the Monkees' CD (1967) with the *Valleri* song I gave you last year. *~ Skipper Mark, Florida*

<u>Jan 3, 2001</u>
De Island boys wuz here, and Irie. We loved every minute of it.

<u>Sept 1, 2001</u>
The Hull Crest School was here too.
What a little slice of paradise. Two days ago, I was skiing in Vermont. Today, I eat Mahi-Mahi. 21st century wonders.

<u>Jan 12, 2001</u>
Thanks for building this place so I could come here. ~ *Gail*

<u>Feb 14, 2001</u>
Bob W. got down on one knee and asked Sandy S. to make an honest man out of him, and she said yes! We got engaged at table 22. Thank you for the hats and champagne!

<u>March 9, 2001</u>
I had an absolutely fabulous time, fun place, great people, and terrific view! Hope to come back again. Love ya, *Gordana, British Columbia.*

We came here and partied all night and we came from aboard the *Virgin Summer*. When we left, what a bummer. Luv ya'll.

<u>April 23, 2001</u>
Back for the second time and it just gets better! Discovered more treasure snorkeling. We'll be back for more next year. (Hopefully!) ~ *Jenny, Chris, Helen, and Jo*

<u>June 2001</u>
To Kevin (the manager)
It was such a pleasure talking to you! Only in a place like this can you see both sunrise and sunset over a herd of goats. ~ *Julie and Eddie*

Kirstie was right, *"Good memories are the greatest treasures of all."*

- 258 -

Chapter 14

Returning to Norman Island
2019

After the closure of the *Billy Bones Beach Bar and Grill,* I never expected to return to Norman Island again.

The memories of the past were filled with sadness and regret, making it difficult for me to think about the island without feeling a sense of loss.

Despite this, I knew that there were countless blessings in my life that I should be grateful for. Two of the biggest blessings were my children, born after the business closed.

Exploring Underwater Treasures

Our son's first dive at the Bight.

In 2019, Dave and I registered our kids for an introductory scuba diving course at *Sail Caribbean Divers.*

Their operation was located at Hodge's Creek Marina on Tortola.

Our kids loved the sea and the opportunity to explore the underwater treasures for the first time was going to be an exciting adventure for all of us, or so I thought.

Our daughter scuba diving at the Bight.

I packed a small bag with towels and sunscreen and drove the winding roads to East End, eager to enroll them in this introductory program. Unbeknownst to me, *Sail Caribbean's* first underwater stop was at the Bight.

As soon as I learned of this, feelings arose that I had never expected, nor prepared for. It had been seventeen years since I left the island, and I wasn't ready to return.

I sat on the boat, unable to alter our destination, and turned inward to listen to the thoughts racing inside my head.

They were looking for a place to escape, *but there was no escape.* I had to face my past.

As we pulled up alongside the familiar dock, I kept my focus on the kids, helping them into their diving gear and allaying their fears.

They were scared and nervous, yet very excited. I was too, but for different reasons.

Once they descended under the water with their instructor, leaving a trail of bubbles in their wake, I took a big breath and headed down the dock to see the island I missed so much.

A Walk Down Memory Lane

To my surprise, as I walked along the dock, I ran into a charter captain that I had known many years ago. He recognized me under my floppy summer hat, and we shared a warm embrace.

The reunion brought a wave of emotion to the surface as we reminisced about the years that had passed since we last saw each other.

We both agreed that seventeen years was a long time. As we chatted, I spotted a familiar face - a waitress that I had missed. She ran down to the dock to greet me and gave me a big hug, which I cherished deeply.

After the emotional reunion, I said goodbye to both with a smile and walked towards the quieter end of the beach, seeking some solitude to reflect on the memories that had surfaced.

As I strolled along the seashore, I remembered the sound of the soft ripples that the waves made against this rocky beach. I recalled the days when I used to watch the seagulls that swirled overhead, fighting for the scraps that the diving pelicans left behind.

Their constant squawks always broke the silence that lingered in the bay, and I loved observing them. Those were the days when there were fewer than a dozen boats anchored in the Bight.

As I gazed out over the horizon, the vastness of the view increased my sense of solitude, feelings echoed by Stevenson himself about his imaginary island.

I hadn't planned to visit Norman Island, but now that I was here, I felt a sense of peace, like a full-circle moment when one returns from where they came from.

Before I knew it, it was time to leave.

A Gift from the Universe

The kids were soon ascending from their dive, and I wanted to be there when they reached the surface to hear all about their first encounter.

A stone found on the beach at Norman Island

As I headed back to the boat, something unusual in the sand caught my eye. I stooped down to pick up the object and was surprised to discover that it was a perfectly formed stone in the shape of a heart.

I couldn't help but feel a sense of wonder and gratitude for this unexpected gift from the universe, particularly at a time when I was feeling vulnerable.

I cherished the find in my hands, another precious token of remembrance, before running back to the boat.

I was just in time to see my daughter emerging from her first dive. She was beaming with excitement and as she climbed aboard, I asked her what she loved most about the experience.

She summed up her feelings perfectly in two sentences.

"Mom, I think I'll always remember the sense of freedom I felt on my very first dive. It was awesome!"

I smiled, feeling a sense of pride, and understanding.

As we took our seats on the shady side of the boat, the mate cast the dock lines aboard, and off we set towards the open sea and home, happy for the unexpected visit to an island that will live on in our hearts forever.

The End.

This poem was written by my grandmother,
a reminder that under each gloomy cloud is always a ray of sunshine.

Faith

There is always a glad tomorrow
After the saddest night.
There is always an end to each sorrow,
And after darkness comes light.

There is always a ray of sunshine,
Under each cloud of gray.
And there's always a song to cheer us along,
For God made it all that way.

There is always a flower growing,
On life's road as we limp along.
There is always a bright face showing,
Amongst the saddest throng.

There is always a cheerful story,
To shorten the days that are long,
And there's always a smile,
To make life worthwhile,
And there's always a right to each wrong.

There is always a heart that is faithful,
Though faithless, the rest of them be.
When all things in this world seem hateful,
There's another world lovelier to see.

There is always a word of comfort,
For a heart burdened down with care,
And there's always another…
It's God's Holy Mother,
Let's take all to her in prayer. ✝
© *Valerie Creque-Mawson*

A Summary

We've come to the end of a journey through six generations of Norman Island's incredible history!

I hope you've enjoyed learning a little more about the island's past through our family's experiences.

The discovery of a hidden treasure is the stuff of legends, and the pursuit of such wealth has captivated people for centuries.

For me, the journey to uncover the story of my ancestor's find began with a series of cryptic clues passed down through the generations.

H.O. Creque's discovery of a stash of precious coins in a musty, bat-filled cave has been a long-held family secret.

The necklace made from the coins found was the tangible proof the story was likely true, confirmed by Peggy and her children.

Recently, one of Peggy's closest friends provided additional evidence to support the rumour by sharing that she had confided in him years ago that *"her family discovered a chest with gold jewelry and papers."*

There is a plaque in Creque's Alley in St. Thomas which reads:

> *"This passage, once known as Creque's Alley, has its own pirate legend. An ancestor of its former owners discovered chests of pirate treasure in a cave on Norman Island.*
>
> *It is rumoured he hid part of it within these premises until it could be converted into bank notes. The fantasy of finding a pirate's hoard and quick wealth still haunts the islands."*

Leaving a Lasting Legacy

This journey has been a thrilling and rewarding experience for me.

It's added depth and richness to my understanding of my family's history and the legacy of my great-great-grandfather's adventurous spirit.

It is a reminder that the discovery of wealth and the desire to leave a lasting legacy are universal human desires that have been present throughout history.

Today, Norman Island is a popular tourist destination, attracting thousands of visitors each year. Many of them come to explore the island's caves, hoping to find a lost treasure themselves.

Whether it was the burial and retrieval of Owen Lloyd's treasure in 1750, or the tales of daring adventures and treasure hunts since then, Norman Island's history endures.

I'm grateful to Robert Louis Stevenson for preserving the legacy of a 1750 tale through his classic novel, *Treasure Island.*

He unknowingly preserved the incredible story about Norman Island, a real *Treasure Island* with pirates and buried treasure.

The End

The Bight ~ 1818

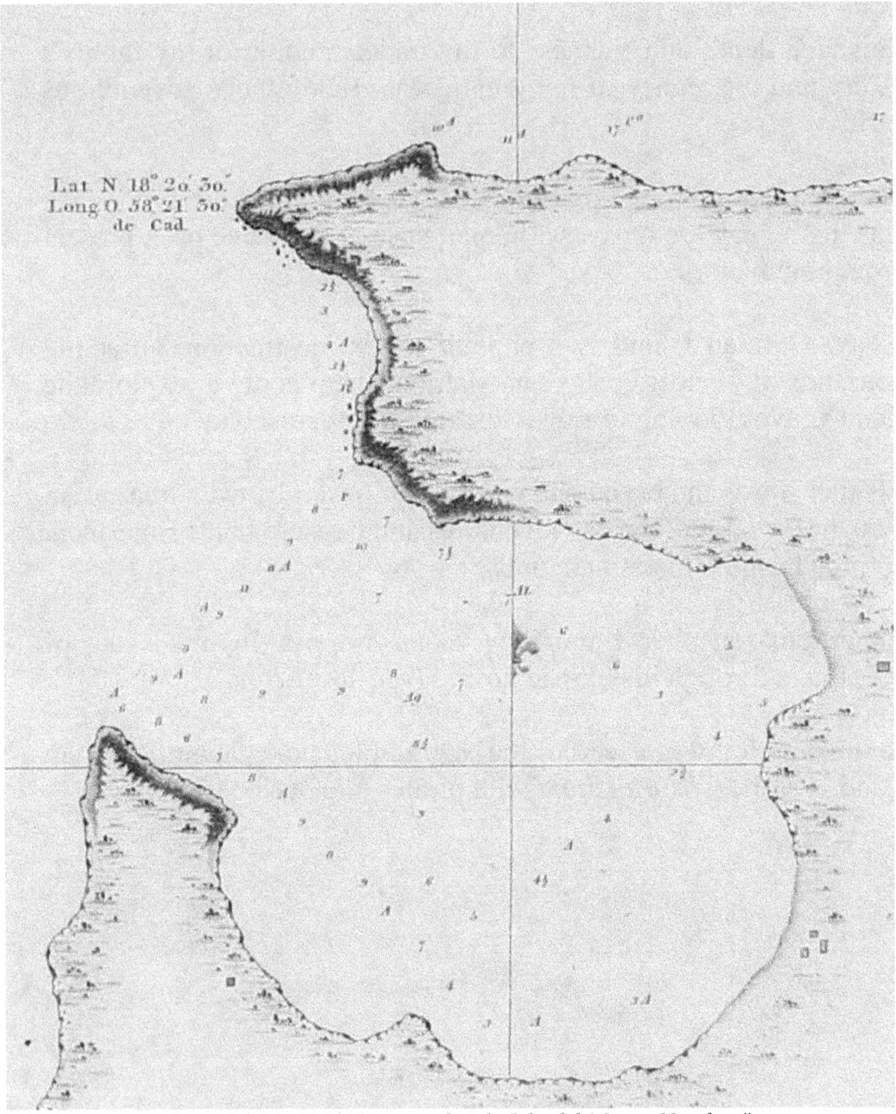

"*Plano del Puerto de Normand en la Isla del Mismo Nombre.*"
© University of Michigan Library Digital Collections.

The Owners of Norman Island
1737 - Present

Below is a list of all the registered owners of Norman Island beginning in the year 1737, a culmination of my research spanning almost thirty years. His Excellency, John Hart, Esq, *Captain General and Governor-in-Chief* of the Leeward Islands granted Norman Island to its first recorded owner.

1.   The Phipps Family, 1737 - 1755

- Governor John Hart granted Norman Island to Colonel Francis Phipps in the year 1737.
- The heirs of Francis Phipps inherited the island in 1751. Constantine Phipps, James Phipps, Edward Phipps, Esq, William Phipps, and Frances Phipps.

2.   The Purcell Family, 1755 - 1799

- John Purcell acquired the island in the year 1755. (He was President of the Virgin Islands in 1752.)
- His heirs, John, Frances, and Margaret Norton Purcell inherited the island in 1771.

3.   The Smith and Hill Families, 1799 - 1817

- John Rogers Smith and Abraham Chalwill Hill ~ The conveyance of a LEASE for the year 1799.
- Mrs. Ann Smith (A relation of John Rogers Smith, advertised Norman Island for sale in the year 1815.)
- Abram Chalwill Hill sold the entire island in 1817, except the use of the house on the bay, and 100 square feet for the duration of his life.

4.   *The Isaacs Family, 1817 - 1827*

- Robert Glover Isaacs acquired the island in 1817.
- His heirs inherited the island, which included William Rogers Isaacs, the Executor in 1823.

5.   *The Patnelli Family, 1827 - 1885*

- George Crabb Patnelli acquired the island in 1827.
- The heirs of G.C. Patnelli inherited the island. - Jenny Patnelli, Mary Patnelli, George Crabb Patnelli, and Amelia Patnelli, Betty Patnelli, Jane Patnelli and George Osmond Patnelli. Ann Jane Patnelli was the Executrix of the estate.

6.   *The Hill Family, 1885 – 1896*

- Mrs. Ann Elizabeth Hill acquired the island by way of a *Deed of Gift* from Ann Jane Patnelli on August 4, 1885.

7.   *The Creque Family, 1896 - 1999*

- Henry Osmond Creque acquired the island on May 19, 1896.
- Herman Ogilvie Creque inherited the island in 1915.
- His widow, Mrs. Emily Creque, inherited the island in 1949.
- Her heirs inherited the island in 1961, and later transferred their shares to Creque Estates, Ltd.

8.   *Audubon Holdings, Ltd., 1999 – Present*

- Audubon Holdings, Ltd. acquired the island in 1999.

Bibliography

Amrhein, John, *Treasure Island: The Untold Story*, New Maritima Press, 2011.

Baird, Charles W., *History of the Huguenot Emigration to America*, Dodd, Mead & Company, New York, 1885. page 209-210.

Benjamin, Hugh, with Myers, Richard B., *A Place Like This*: *Hugh Benjamin's Peter Island*, Two Thousand Three Associates, 1994.

Carstens, J.L., *St. Thomas in Early Danish Times, A General Description of all the Danish, American or West Indian Islands, 1740-1780*, translated by Arnold R. Highfield, The Virgin Islands Humanities Council, St. Croix, 1997.

Chenoweth, John M., *Simplicity, Equality, and Slavery: An Archaeology of Quakerism in the British Virgin Islands*, Florida Museum of Natural History: Ripley P. Buller Series. 2017.

Cochran, Hamilton, *These are the Virgin Islands*, Prentice Hall, Inc., New York, 1937.

Cordingly, David, and Falconer, John, *Pirates: Fact and Fiction*, Royal Museums Greenwich, London, 1992.

Cordingly, David, *Under the Black Flag*, Mariner Books, London, 1997.

Dookhan, Isaac, *A History of the British Virgin Islands*, University Press of the West Indies, 1994.

Fenger, Frederic, *Alone in the Caribbean*, George H. Doran Company, New York, 1917.

Fenger, Frederic, *The Golden Parrot*, Houghton Mifflin, Boston, Mass., 1921.

Harman, Jeanne Perkins, *The Love Junk*, Appleton-Century Corp, New York, 1951.

Horner, Dave, *The Treasure Galleons*, Florida Classics, 1990.

Irving, Washington, *Tales of a Traveler*, John Murray, London, 1824.

Johnson, Charles, Captain *A General History of the Robberies and Murders of the Most Notorious Pirates*, New York, 1724.

Kent, Michael D., *Twice She Struck, The Story of RMS Rhone*, Michael D. Kent, 2017.

Kingsley, Charles, *At Last: A Christmas in the West Indies*, Harper and Brothers, New York, 1871.

Marryat, Frederick, *Masterman Ready*, A.L. Burt Company, New York, 1898.

Mathewson, R. Duncan, Fisher, Mel, *Treasure of the Atocha: A Four Hundred Dollar Archaeological Adventure*, Pisces Books, E.P. Dutton, 1986.

Mawson, Valerie Creque, *Poems from a Small Island*, Posterity Press, Chevy Chase, Maryland, 2009.

O'Neal, Joseph Reynold, *Life Notes, Reflections of a British Virgin Islander*, U.S. Xlibris Corporation, 2004.

Paine, Ralph D., *The Book of Buried Treasure*, Arno Press, New York, 1981.

Personius, Mark, *An Assessment of the Development Potential for Norman Island, BVI*, University of Minnesota, Department of Geography, 1989.

Putley, Julian, *The Virgins' Treasure Isle*, Virgin Island Books, 2010.

Rodgers, Bradley A., Cantelas; Frank, Richards; Nathan; Corbin, Annalies; Seltzer, Erica; Pietruszka, Andrew; Meverden, Keith; Seeb, Sami, and Weir, Andrew; *Shipwrecks of St. John, ECU Investigations of Submerged Cultural Resources in the U.S. Virgin Islands National Park*, Research Report No 16., 2002.

Sedwick, Daniel, and Sedwick, Frank, *The Practical Book of Cobs*, Third edition, Daniel Frank Sedwick, LLC., 1995.

Seyfarth, Fritz, *The Pirates of the Virgin Islands*, Spanish Main Press, 1986.

Shomette, Donald G., *Shipwrecks, Sea Raiders and Maritime Disasters Along the Delmarva Coast*, Johns Hopkins University Press, 2007.

Sims, Valerie, *Vintage St. John: Discover St. John's History Through Seven Generations of Heartfelt Stories*, Vintage World Media, SEC., 2020.

Southey, Thomas, *A Chronological History of the West Indies, Vol III,* page 361, 1827.

Tattersall, Jill, *Stolen Treasures of the Caribbean*, Island Legends, British Virgin Islands, 1993.

Tattersall, Jill, *Captain Kidd in the Virgin Islands,* Island Legends, British Virgin Islands.

Teytaud, A.R., *A Study of Management Alternatives for the Proposed Protected Areas at Sandy Cay and Norman Island*, B.V.I., 1983.

Unknown, *Letters from the Virgin Islands, Illustrating Life and Manners in the West Indies,* London, 1843.

van Marle, Quentin, *Marooned, One Man's Ordeal on Dead Man's Chest, 31 Days on Blackbeard's Island*, New Nautilus Press, 1995.

Wilkins, Harold T., *Pirate Treasure*, E.P. Dutton & Co., New York, 1937.

Discover St. John's History!

Vintage St. John

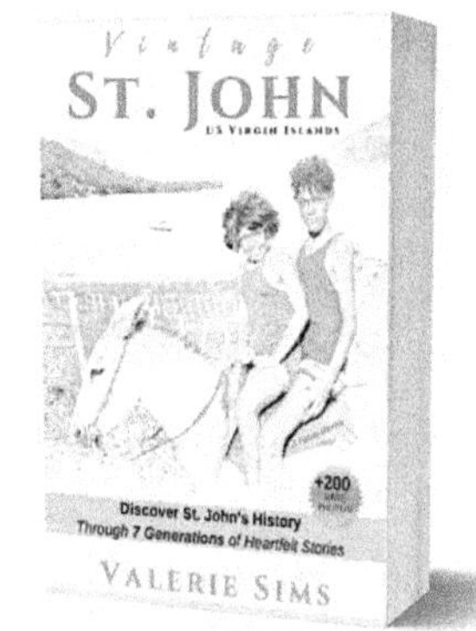

When a prominent St. Thomas merchant accumulates 2,500 acres on the island of St. John to raise cattle and cultivate bay leaves, he has no idea that his generation will be the last to farm the land.

During the 1920s to the 1950s, Herman O. Creque's hard work pays off on his estates of Annaberg, Mary's Point, and Lamesure, but at the peak of their profitability, he dies, leaving them all to his wife, Emily.

Summer Fun at Francis Bay

Francis Bay is their children's favorite with almost thirty years of summer memories, fishing, hunting, and crabbing. One day, the beach and summer cottage will be theirs, *or so they believe.*

Laurance Rockefeller and Frank Stick

When two conservationists from the United States visit the island in 1952, they find the unspoiled nature of Emily's lands enchanting and wish to preserve them for *"the enjoyment of the nation."*

Little do Emily's children suspect that life as they know it is about to change, and the UNTHINKABLE will tear their family apart.

The Virgin Islands National Park

Vintage St. John is a collection of their heartfelt memories, woven together from personal interviews. They paint a vivid picture of life before the establishment of the Virgin Islands National Park… *and life shortly after.*   VintageStJohnbook.com

ORDER YOUR COPY FROM AMAZON TODAY!

Acknowledgements

I would like to express my sincerest gratitude to several individuals and organizations who in one way or another, contributed to the successful publication of this manuscript.

I am forever grateful to my mother, Marlene Carney for encouraging me to document these stories and bring them to life. I'm so thankful to her and to her husband, Bob Malacarne, and my sister, Leslie Carney as well for their steadfast support and encouragement.

To my husband, David Sims, and our children who have endured the ups and downs of this writing journey, thank you for your untiring patience and understanding. I love you!

I'm especially appreciative to those who provided the additional stories, photographs, digital images, and documents shared within these pages, namely: The rare photographs of Thomas Dixon Green and his son, David Green of Tortola and the UK, and the kindness of Mrs. Jane Steen of *The Sheen Collection* in St. Thomas.

Also, Herman and Emily Creque, Valerie Creque-Mawson, Leon A. Mawson, Richard and Marion Miller, Charles C. Selby, William (Bill) Creque, Juliette Creque Scobie, Henry O. Creque and Margaret (Peggy) Creque, John Bedford Creque, Henry Owen Creque, IV, Frank and Alda Creque, Inez Turnbull, David W. Knight, Sr., Dr. Dante Beretta, Mrs. Verna Penn Moll, Philip Sturm, Jill Tattersall, and Mrs. Janice Nibbs Blyden.

Thank you to the National Archives in the UK, the Royal Danish Library in Copenhagen, Denmark, the National Archives in Washington, DC, the Archives of the British Virgin Islands, The Virgin Islands Daily News, Ancestry.com, FamilySearch.org, the Enid M. Baa Library, the Elaine Ione Sprauve Library, the Charles W. Turnbull Regional Library in the US Virgin Islands, and the always helpful librarian there, Miss Beverly Smith.

In addition, I would like to thank the Billy Bones staff for all of their hard work and dedication and for the fun times we shared working together. My apologies to anyone who's name I may have missed.

Kitchen Staff: Uneida, Martina, Laura, Denise, Monica, Andrea, Pam, Yellow Man, Dahlia
Bartenders: Kidd, Randy, Rachel, Andy, April, Ian, Jayme, Ross, Grant, Collin
Wait Staff: Jessica, Rosie, Sally, Pet, Esther, Grace, Dillon
Office: Theresa, Marva, Jenny
Gift Shop: Sandra, Shernelle
Managers: Duane, Kirstie, Kevin
Boat Captain: Everton

I couldn't have shared these memories and stories without everyone's contributions.

Thank you! 🌸

About the Author

Valerie's love of family history all started with wonderful conversations with her grandmother!

Her entertaining tales of buried treasures, haunted houses, and out-of-body experiences sent shivers down her spine and sparked her life-long fascination with genealogy.

In 2010, Valerie captured the top prize for the *Deputy Governor's History Research Award* in the British Virgin Islands for her research paper about her second great-grandfather. It was entitled, *The Life of Henry O. Creque, 1858 to 1915, A Biography.*

In 2015, she began researching and writing for her blog *VintageVirginIslands.com.* Today, it hosts over 300 posts about the history of the US Virgin Islands, the Danish West Indies, and the British Virgin Islands.

In 2020, she published her first book about the history of the island of St. John entitled, *Vintage St. John, Discover St. John's History Through Seven Generations of Heartfelt Stories.*

Vintage Norman Island is her second family memoir. She hopes it will inspire others to document their family stories and keep their heritage alive.

In 2023, she'll be offering a 6-week program to help family historians publish their family memoirs, sharing her tips and templates. It's called *From Piles of Files to Published™.*

Learn more at *PublishYourFamilyHistory*.com and download a free guide to get started.

Valerie and her husband currently make their home in the Caribbean, raising their two children with a watchful eye on their two little dogs.

Valerie Sims

Follow Valerie on the Web!

If you've enjoyed this book, please send me a message. I would love to hear from you! I'm on Facebook every day, so you can connect me there:

- Email address: VintageVI@icloud.com

- Follow me on Facebook with 9,500+ fans at Facebook.com/VintageVirginIslands

- For book purchases, visit: NormanIslandBook.com

Vintage Norman Island is available on amazon.com, and selected retail stores in the US and British Virgin Islands.

For more stories about Norman Island, visit VintageNormanIsland.com

Now that this fun project is completed, I'm working on another exciting one!

Sign up here for updates: ValerieSims.com/newsletter/

If you enjoyed this book and have a minute, I would greatly appreciate your review on amazon's platform to help the book's ranking. It's the best way of showing your support!

Thank you so much!

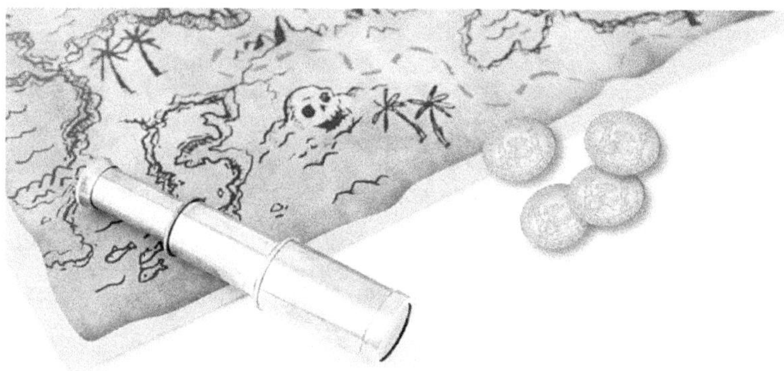

The Hunt for Hidden Treasure

Norman Island, with a treasure trove untold,
Where pirates roamed in the days of old.

With Captain Lloyd in command, the pirates hit land,
To bury their loot before anyone could snoop.

In Money Bay, where the treasure lay,
Deeply buried until one day.

The people of Tortola searched and dug,
With pick and spade where the treasure laid.

Silver and coins, a glittering sight,
The haul of a lifetime, a treasure so bright.

But the island's secrets are not yet done,
For more treasure awaits, under the sun.

So if you're a pirate, with a heart full of dreams,
Set sail for Norman Island, where treasures beam.

But be aware of other pirates too,
Who seek hidden treasures, just like you!

Index

A

B

C

D

E

F

*If history were taught in
the form of stories,*

IT WOULD NEVER BE FORGOTTEN

~ Rudyard Kipling